Praise for
Lazarus Awakening

"Joanna Weaver has done it again! By revealing the profound love Jesus had for Lazarus and the shocking life-after-death-on-earth He lavished on His friend, she skillfully points the reader to a vibrant choice—*abundant life!* If you long to wake up to God's unrestricted mercy, unconditional love, and supernatural power, read this book!"

> —CAROL KENT, speaker and author of *Between a Rock
> and a Grace Place*

"I sat down to read *Lazarus Awakening* and quickly realized this wasn't going to be a fluffy read I'd soon forget. I needed a pen and a journal and time to take notes. *Lazarus Awakening* is full of life-changing truth and application. Through Joanna's beautiful teaching, God is calling us all to resurrected life!"

> —ANGELA THOMAS, speaker and best-selling author
> of *Do You Know Who I Am?*

"*Lazarus Awakening* firmly establishes Joanna Weaver as one of the finest Christian writers of our time. Spiritually insightful, personally compelling, and magnificently written, this is one of the best books I've read in decades. We know she's walking the journey she's inviting us to take. I believe *Lazarus Awakening* will awaken many more believers to this extraordinarily gifted author."

> —DONNA PARTOW, speaker and best-selling author
> of *Becoming a Vessel God Can Use*

"The word that wouldn't leave me when reading *Lazarus Awakening* is *deep.* Joanna Weaver's words are rooted deep in Scripture, they dove deep into my heart, and they deeply impacted my emotions as I've come to a better understanding that Jesus loves me because of who I am, not what I've done. I cried many tears through these pages as my own questions were tackled, my own fears revealed. In the end I've come away with a deeper understanding of what it means to be loved by God. I am blessed, I am loved, and Jesus means more to me than ever before."

> —TRICIA GOYER, author of *Blue Like Play Dough*

"If you worry that you are unworthy of God's favor or you wonder why He doesn't intervene to prevent your pain, *Lazarus Awakening* will take you straight to the heart of His love for you. With warmth, honesty, and rich biblical insights, Joanna Weaver deftly walks you through the agony of the loss and the triumph of resurrection to reveal how friendship with Jesus makes all the difference."

—JENNIFER ROTHSCHILD, author of *Lessons I Learned in the Dark*
and *Me, Myself, and Lies* and founder of WomensMinistry.net

"I needed to read this book. You need to read this book. Sometimes we can get stuck in sin-sickness, living a Christian life that is neither glorious nor free. Joanna Weaver reminds us of all that Jesus offers us when we step out of the tomb of our own making into the joyous life He has created us for. *Lazarus Awakening* awakened something in me."

—SUSANNA FOTH AUGHTMON, author of *My Bangs Look Good*
and Other Lies I Tell Myself

"Joanna Weaver has given us two insightful books about some of Jesus's closest friends—Martha and Mary. *Lazarus Awakening* completes the trilogy by taking an inspiring look at the life of their brother, Lazarus. A closer look at his story will help you draw closer to Christ as His intimate friend. I recommend it."

—ANN SPANGLER, author of *Praying the Names of God*

Lazarus
Awakening

JOANNA WEAVER

Finding Your Place
in the Heart *of* God

Lazarus Awakening

WATERBROOK
PRESS

LAZARUS AWAKENING
PUBLISHED BY WATERBROOK PRESS
12265 Oracle Boulevard, Suite 200
Colorado Springs, Colorado 80921

All Scripture quotations, unless otherwise indicated, are taken from the Holy Bible, New International Version®. NIV®. Copyright © 1973, 1978, 1984 by Biblica Inc.™ Used by permission of Zondervan. All rights reserved worldwide. www.zondervan.com. Scripture quotations marked (DRA) are from the Douay-Rheims 1899 American edition, published by the John Murphy Company, Baltimore, Maryland. Accessed through Bible Gateway, www.biblegateway.com/versions/Douay-Rheims-1899-American-Edition-DRA-Bible/#copy. Scripture quotations marked (KJV) are taken from the King James Version. Scripture quotations marked (MSG) are taken from The Message by Eugene H. Peterson. Copyright © 1993, 1994, 1995, 1996, 2000, 2001, 2002. Used by permission of NavPress Publishing Group. All rights reserved. Scripture quotation marked (NCV) are taken from the New Century Version®. Copyright © 1987, 1988, 1991 by Thomas Nelson Inc. Used by permission. All rights reserved. Scripture quotations marked (NKJV) are taken from the New King James Version®. Copyright © 1982 by Thomas Nelson Inc. Used by permission. All rights reserved. Scripture quotations marked (NLT) are taken from the Holy Bible, New Living Translation, copyright © 1996, 2004. Used by permission of Tyndale House Publishers Inc., Wheaton, Illinois 60189. All rights reserved.

Personal stories appearing in this book are used by permission. In some instances the names or details have been changed to protect the privacy of the persons involved.

ISBN 978-0-307-44496-7
ISBN 978-0-307-44497-4 (electronic)

Jacket design by Mark D. Ford; photograph by Susan Friedman/Graphistock

Published in association with the literary agency of Janet Kobobel Grant, Books & Such, 5926 Sunhawk Drive, Santa Rosa, CA 95409.

Published in the United States by WaterBrook Multnomah, an imprint of the Crown Publishing Group, a division of Random House Inc., New York.

WATERBROOK and its deer colophon are registered trademarks of Random House Inc.

Library of Congress Cataloging-in-Publication Data
Weaver, Joanna.
    Lazarus awakening : finding your place in the heart of God / Joanna Weaver. — 1st ed.
        p. cm.
    Includes bibliographical references.
    ISBN 978-0-307-44496-7 — ISBN 978-0-307-44497-4 (electronic)
    1. Lazarus, of Bethany, Saint. 2. Raising of Lazarus (Miracle) 3. Bible. N.T. John XI-XII, 1-11—Criticism, interpretation, etc. 4. God (Christianity)—Love. I. Title.
    BS2460.L3W43 2011
    226.5'06—dc22
                            2010037933

Printed in the United States of America
2011—First Edition

10 9 8 7 6 5 4 3 2 1

SPECIAL SALES
Most WaterBrook Multnomah books are available at special quantity discounts when purchased in bulk by corporations, organizations, and special-interest groups. Custom imprinting or excerpting can also be done to fit special needs. For information, please e-mail SpecialMarkets@WaterBrookMultnomah.com or call 1-800-603-7051.

To my father, Cliff Gustafson.
Passionate follower and friend of Jesus Christ,
lover of people,
unwinder of graveclothes.

Daddy,
I met Jesus the day I met you.
Thank you for living your life out loud for God.
I'm so honored to be your daughter.

Lord! We entreat you,

make us truly alive.

SERAPION OF THMUIS (FOURTH CENTURY)

Contents

Acknowledgments   xiii

1   Tale of the Third Follower   2

2   Lord, the One You Love Is Sick   18

3   Our Friend Lazarus   32

4   When Love Tarries   50

5   Tomb Dwelling   66

6   Roll Away the Stone   84

7   When Love Calls Your Name   102

8   Unwinding Graveclothes   120

9   Living Resurrected   138

10   Laughing Lazarus   156

Appendix A: The Story (John 11:1–12:11)   175

Appendix B: Study Guide   179

Appendix C: Resources for Resurrected Living   197

Appendix D: Who I Am in Christ   201

Appendix E: Identifying Strongholds   203

Appendix F: Hints for Unwinding Graveclothes   207

Notes   211

Acknowledgments

I've been told that before starting a musical composition, Johann Sebastian Bach would write two letters at the top of the score: *J.J.,* which stood for *Jesu Juva.* "Jesus, help." Those two words have been my daily prayer, and if this book ministers to you in any way, it is all due to Jesus Christ—my Helper and my Friend. More than ever before, I'm discovering the truth of these words: "Without Him, I can do nothing."

But I'm also grateful to a family who has loved and supported me through the process. To my dear parents, Cliff and Annette Gustafson. Thank you for interceding daily for me and this book and for making your house so much fun that at times Joshua didn't want to leave! To my older kids—Jessica, John Michael, and my precious new daughter-in-love, Kami—thank you for the encouraging text messages and phone prayers that carried me through. And to my husband, John. There just aren't enough words. I can't imagine who I'd be, let alone where I'd be, without you.

To all my dear friends at church and online who have lifted this book in prayer, especially Lorene Masters, Donna Partow, Jodi Detrick, Sherrie Snyder, and Angela Howard, thank you. Along with the others, your intercession literally put words on the page at times. Special thanks to Randy and Kay Creech for your friendship and generous hospitality. And to Shantel Watson and others who dropped off delicious meals and provided play dates for Josh.

To Wendy Lawton, whose insightful words—"It *is* a book"—launched the whole process of writing the story of Lazarus. You have my gratitude for being God's voice to my heart.

Without Laura Barker, Carol Bartley, and the amazing team of people at Water-Brook, this book wouldn't have been possible. Thank you for your extravagant patience and for believing in this book. You have been so gracious. May God richly bless each and every one of you.

To Anne Christian Buchanan. Thank you for helping me prune and shape my ideas and words. A skilled editor is truly a gift to a writer, and what a gift you've been to me. I thank God for you.

Finally, to Janet Kobobel Grant, my agent. Two are better than one, the Bible says, and oh how that's true of this author. Thank you for seeing something in me so many years ago and walking beside me every step of the way. I am blessed to have you in my life.

When Bach finished a piece of music, he would write another set of letters at the bottom of the page: *S.D.G.—Soli Deo Gloria,* which means "glory to God alone."

That is my prayer for this book as well.

Soli Deo Gloria.

Now a man named Lazarus was sick.
He was from Bethany, the village of
Mary and her sister Martha. This Mary,
whose brother Lazarus now lay sick,
was the same one who poured perfume on the Lord
and wiped his feet with her hair.
So the sisters sent word to Jesus, "Lord, the one you love is sick."

JOHN 11:1–3

seem to change what one friend calls an epidemic among Christian women (and many men as well): a barren heart condition I call love-doubt.

"Jesus loves me—this I know, for the Bible tells me so."[1] Many of us have sung the song since we were children. But do we really believe it? Or has Christ's love remained more of a fairy tale than a reality we've experienced for ourselves in the only place we can really know for sure?

Our hearts.

What Kind of Father Do You Have?

So much of our understanding of God's love is shaped by what we've experienced in life. Those who are abused or misused as children often struggle with the thought of God as a loving Parent, and even those raised in healthy homes can have distorted views of their heavenly Father. Which of the following misrepresentations are you most likely to struggle with?

Abusive Father: You never know what you are going to get with this kind of father. Will he be nice when he walks in, or will he hit you upside the head first chance he gets? His love is determined by his moods. You avoid him as much as possible.

> *But your true Father* is "gracious and compassionate, slow to anger and rich in love" (Psalm 145:8).

Neglectful Father: This dad is far too busy (or just too selfish) to be concerned with you. He's got bigger, more important business to attend to than your insignificant needs. While he may be present in your life, he's largely unaccounted for. You have to take care of yourself.

> *But your true Father says,* "Look at the birds of the air; they do not sow or reap or store away in barns, and yet your

Tale of the
Third Follower

It's amazing that such a little space could make so much difference.

Just eighteen inches, give or take a few—that's all it needs to move. And yet, for many of us, getting God's love from our heads to our hearts may be the most difficult—yet the most important—thing we ever attempt to do.

"I need to talk," Lisa whispered in my ear one day after women's Bible study. A committed Christian with a deep passion for the Lord, my friend had tears pooling in her dark eyes as we found a quiet corner where we could talk.

"I don't know what's wrong with me," she said, shaking her head as she looked down at her feet. "I could go to the worst criminal or a drug addict living on the street, and I could look him in the eye and tell him, 'Jesus loves you!' and mean it from the bottom of my heart.

"But, Joanna," she said, gripping my hand, "I can't seem to look in the mirror and convince myself."

Her words were familiar to me. I'd felt that same terrible disconnect early in my walk with the Lord. Hoping He loved me but never really knowing for sure. Sadly, I've heard the same lonely detachment echoed by hundreds of women I've talked to around the country. Beautiful women. Plain women. Talented and not-so-talented women. Strong Christian women, deep in the Word and active in their church, as well as women brand new to their faith. Personal attributes or IQs seem to matter little. Whether they were raised in a loving home or an abusive situation, it doesn't

He Loves Me...He Loves Me Not

You would think after accepting Christ at a young age and being raised in a loving Christian home with a loving, gracious father, I would have been convinced from the beginning that my heavenly Father loved me.

Me. With all my faults and failures. My silly stubbornness and pride.

But those very things kept me from really knowing Christ's love for the majority

---

heavenly Father feeds them. Are you not much more valuable than they?" (Matthew 6:26).

Biased Father: You know this father loves you—or at least you think he does. But he seems to shower affection and gifts on all the other kids, leaving you with leftovers and hand-me-downs. Bottom line: he has favorites, and you're not one of them. You had better get used to it.

But your true Father "does not show favoritism" (Romans 2:11).

Demanding Father: Perfect in nearly every way, this father demands that you be perfect as well. No matter how hard you try, it's never enough. While there are moments when he seems proud of you, they are few and far between. Instead, you carry a heavy sense of his disapproval.

But your true Father "has compassion on his children...for he knows how we are formed, he remembers that we are dust" (Psalm 103:13–14).

How great is the love the Father has lavished on us,
that we should be called children of God! And that is what we are!

1 John 3:1

of my early adult life. There was just so much to dislike, so much to disapprove of. How could God possibly love me? Even *I* wasn't that crazy about me.

For some reason, I'd come to see God as distant and somewhat removed. Rather than transposing upon God the model of my earthly father's balanced love—both unconditional yet corrective—I saw my heavenly Father as a stern teacher with a yardstick in His hand, pacing up and down the classroom of my life as He looked for any and all infractions. Measuring me against what sometimes felt like impossible standards and occasionally slapping me when I failed to make the grade.

Yes, He loved me, I supposed. At least that's what I'd been taught. But I didn't always feel God's love. Most of the time I lived in fear of the yardstick. Who knew when His judgment would snap down its disapproval, leaving a nasty mark on my heart as well as my soul?

As a result, I lived the first three decades of my life like an insecure adolescent, forever picking daisies and tearing them apart, never stopping to enjoy their beauty. *He loves me, He loves me not,* I would say subconsciously, plucking a petal as I weighed my behavior and attitudes against what the Bible said I should be.

Powerful church services and sweet altar times. Ah, I felt secure in His love. Real life and less-than-sweet responses? I felt lost and all alone. Unfortunately, all I got from constantly questioning God's love was a fearful heart and a pile of torn, wilted petals. My overzealous self-analysis never brought the peace I longed for.

Because the peace you and I were created for doesn't come from picking daisies. It only comes from a living relationship with a loving God.

THE TALE OF THE THIRD FOLLOWER

I never planned on writing a trilogy about Mary, Martha, and Lazarus, the siblings from Bethany that we meet in Luke's and John's gospels. In fact, when I wrote *Having a Mary Heart in a Martha World,* I was fairly certain it was the one and only book to be found in those verses. But God surprised me six years later, and *Having a Mary Spirit* was born.

The thought that there might be a third book never crossed my mind until I shared an interesting premise with a few friends who are writers. It was a teaching point I'd hoped to fit into *Having a Mary Spirit* but never quite found room.

"We all know Jesus loved Mary," I told my friends. "After all, look how she worshiped. And we can even understand how Jesus loved Martha. Look how she served. But what about those of us who don't know where we fit in the heart of God?"

The question hung in the air before I continued.

"The only thing of significance that Lazarus did was die. And yet when Mary and Martha sent word to Jesus that Lazarus was ill, they said, 'Lord, the one you *love* is sick.' "

Somehow my words seemed to have extra weight as they floated between us. Extra importance. Even I felt their impact.

After a few moments my friend Wendy broke the silence. "That part of the story didn't make it into the book because *it is* a book."

I can't adequately explain what happened when she said those words, except to say it was as though a giant bell began to sound in my soul. Its reverberations sent shock waves through my body as I tried to change the subject.

The thing is, I didn't *want* to write about Lazarus. I wanted to write a different book. I was ready to move on, to explore other subjects.

But God wouldn't let me. And so you hold this book in your hands.

A PLACE TO CALL HOME

We first meet the family from Bethany in Luke 10:38–42. Or rather we meet part of the family—two followers of Jesus named Martha and Mary.

You're probably familiar with the story Luke tells. Jesus was on His way to Jerusalem for one of the great Jewish feasts when Martha came out to meet Him with an invitation to dinner. But while Martha opened her home, it was her sister, Mary, who opened her heart. To put the story in a nutshell: Mary worshiped. Martha complained. Jesus rebuked. And lives were changed.[2]

Strangely, Luke's account never even mentions Mary and Martha's brother, Lazarus. Perhaps he wasn't home when Martha held her dinner party. Perhaps he was away on business. Or perhaps he was there all the time but no one really noticed.

Some people are like that. They have perfected the art of invisibility. Experts at fading into the background, they go out of their way not to attract attention, and when they get noticed, they feel great discomfort.

Of course, I have no way of knowing if this was true of Lazarus. Scripture doesn't give any information as to who he was or what he was like—only that he lived in Bethany and had two sisters. When we finally meet him, in John 11, it is an odd introduction—for it starts with a 911 call that leads to a funeral:

> Now a man named Lazarus was sick. He was from Bethany, the village of
> Mary and her sister Martha. This Mary, whose brother Lazarus now lay sick,
> was the same one who poured perfume on the Lord and wiped his feet with
> her hair. So the sisters sent word to Jesus, "Lord, the one you love is sick."
>
> When he heard this, Jesus said, "This sickness will not end in death. No,
> it is for God's glory so that God's Son may be glorified through it." Jesus
> loved Martha and her sister and Lazarus. Yet when he heard that Lazarus
> was sick, he stayed where he was two more days.
>
> Then he said to his disciples, "Let us go back to Judea."....
>
> On his arrival, Jesus found that Lazarus had already been in the tomb for
> four days....
>
> ..."Where have you laid him?" he asked.
>
> "Come and see, Lord," they replied.
>
> Jesus wept. (John 11:1–7, 17, 34–35)

What a tender story. A story filled with emotion and dramatic tension. The story of two sisters torn by grief and a Savior who loved them yet chose to tarry.

Of course, there is more to it—more truths we'll discover as we walk through the forty-four verses John devotes to this tale. For the story of Lazarus is also the story of Jesus's greatest miracle: that of awakening His friend from the dead. (To read the whole story all at once, see Appendix A: "The Story.")

Have you noticed that when Jesus comes on the scene, what seems to be the end is rarely the end? In fact, it's nearly always a new beginning.

But Mary and Martha didn't know that at the time. And I'm prone to forget it as well.

Questions and disappointments, sorrow and fear tend to block out the bigger picture in situations like the one we see in Bethany. What do we do when God doesn't come through the way we hoped He would? What should we feel when what is dearest to our hearts is suddenly snatched away? How do we reconcile the love of God with the disappointments we face in life?

Such questions don't have easy answers. However, in this story of Jesus's three friends, I believe we can find clues to help us navigate the unknown and the tragic when we encounter them in our own lives. Tips to help us live in the *mean*time— that cruel in-between time when we are waiting for God to act—as well as insights to help us trust Him when He doesn't seem to be doing anything at all.

But most important, I believe the story of Lazarus reveals the scandalous availability of God's love if we will only reach out and accept it. Even when we don't deserve it. Even when life is hard and we don't understand.

For God's ways are higher than our ways, and His thoughts are higher than our thoughts, Isaiah 55:8–9 tells us. He knows what He's doing.

Even when we can't figure out His math.

ALGEBRA AND ME

Arithmetic was always one of my favorite subjects in grade school, one I excelled at. Of course, that was in the last century, before they started introducing algebra in kindergarten. In my post–*Leave It to Beaver,* yet very serene, childhood, the only equations that wrinkled my nine-year-old forehead were fairly straightforward:

$$2 + 2 = 4$$
$$19 - 7 = 12$$

Of course, fourth-grade math was more difficult than that. But the basic addition and subtraction skills I'd learned in first and second grade helped me tackle the multiplication and division problems of third and fourth grade with confidence. By the time I reached sixth grade, I was fairly proficient with complicated columns of sums and had pretty much conquered the mysterious world of fractions. I was amazing—a math whiz.

But then eighth grade dawned and, with it, a very brief introduction to algebra. It all seemed quite silly to me. Who cared what the y factor was? And why on earth would I ever need to know what $x + y + z$ equaled?

When my teacher gave us a high-school placement math exam that spring, I didn't spend a lot of time trying to figure out the answers—mainly because I had no idea how, and when I tried, it made my head hurt. Instead, when I encountered a difficult problem during the test, I did what had always worked for me: I looked for a pattern in the answers.

Allowing my mind to back up a bit and my eyes to go a little fuzzy, I'd stare at all those little ovals I'd so neatly darkened in with my number-two pencil until I could see a pattern. *I haven't filled in a D for a while.* Or, *There were two Bs and then two Cs and one A, so obviously this must be another A.*

I was amazing at this too.

No, really, I was. Several weeks later when we received the results of our testing, I had been placed not in bonehead math, not even in beginning algebra. No, it was accelerated algebra for me, though I hadn't a clue what I was doing.

To this day I still don't. My algebraic cluelessness has followed me through adulthood and on into parenting. My kids can ask an English question, quiz me on history or government, and I can usually give them an answer or at least help them find one. But when it comes to algebra or geometry or calculus or any of those other advanced math classes invented by some sick, twisted Einstein wannabe…well, they'd better go ask their dad.

Advanced mathematics remains a complete mystery to me. The unknown factors seem so haphazard. What if z/y squared doesn't equal nine? What then?

The unknown factors frustrate us in life's story problems as well—and there are plenty of those in John 11. How are we to compute the fact that Jesus stayed where He was rather than rushing to Lazarus's side when He heard His friend was ill? How do we reconcile Jesus's allowing Mary and Martha to walk through so much pain when He could have prevented it in the first place?

Difficult questions, without a doubt. But there is a foundational truth in this passage we must first acknowledge before we can tackle the tougher issues.

"Jesus *loved* Martha and her sister and Lazarus" (John 11:5, emphasis added).

Jesus loves you and me as well. He loves us just as we are—apart from our Martha works and Mary worship. He even loves those of us who come empty-handed, feeling dead inside and perhaps a little bound.

For while it may not add up in our human calculations, the truth of God's love lies at the heart of the gospel. "While we were still sinners," Romans 5:8 tells us, "Christ died for us." We may not be able to do the math ourselves or reason out such amazing grace, but if we'll simply ask, our heavenly Father longs to help us find the bottom line.

The Lazarus Factor

I've always told my husband, John, that he has to die before I do—mainly because I don't want him remarrying some wonderful woman and finding out what he's missed all these years. But then again, if he were to go first, I'm convinced I'd face financial ruin in two months. It's not because John hasn't taken very good care of us financially but because I absolutely hate balancing checkbooks.

My idea of reconciling my checking account is to call a very nice lady named Rhonda at our bank. She graciously lets me know the bottom line whenever I'm a little leery of where I stand.

Now, I know this isn't a wise way to handle fiscal matters. In fact, you CPAs reading this are about to faint if you haven't already thrown the book across the room. But, hey, it works for me.

Most of the time.

Okay, so there have been a few blips in my system. But I'm coming to believe that while this may not be such a great method in the natural realm, it may be the only way to go in the spiritual.

After spending the greater part of my life trying to make everything add up on my own—that is, trying to make sure my good outweighed my bad so I was never overdrawn but was continually making deposits in my righteousness bank—I finally realized that nothing I did could ever be enough. No matter how hard I tried, I constantly lived under the weight of my own disapproval. Which, of course, instantly mutated into a sense that God was coldly disappointed with me as well.

He loves me not...

Keeping my own spiritual books has never added up to anything but guilt and condemnation and an overwhelming sense of hopelessness. I'm so glad God's math isn't like mine. And oh how I rejoice that He doesn't demand I come up with the correct answer before He makes me His child. Because when I couldn't make it up to Him, Jesus came down to me. And through His precious blood sacrifice, He made a way for me to come not only into His presence but directly into the heart of God.

"All of this is a gift from God," 2 Corinthians 5:18–19 tells us, "who brought

Holding Out for Grace

I appreciate what Bono, the lead singer of the rock group U2, has to say about grace: "It's a mind-blowing concept that the God who created the Universe might be looking for company, a real relationship with people, but the thing that keeps me on my knees is the difference between Grace and Karma."[3]

Bono explains that the idea of karma is central to all religions:

What you put out comes back to you: an eye for an eye, a tooth for a tooth, or in physics—in physical laws—every action is met by an equal or an opposite one. It's clear to me that Karma is at the very heart of the Universe. I'm absolutely sure of it. And yet, along comes this idea called Grace to upend all that "As you reap, so you will sow" stuff. Grace defies reason and logic. Love interrupts, if you like, the consequences of your actions, which in my case is very good news indeed, because I've done a lot of stupid stuff.… It doesn't excuse my mistakes, but I'm holding out for Grace. I'm holding out that Jesus took my sins onto the Cross, because I know who I am, and I hope I don't have to depend on my own religiosity.[4]

There is no God like you. You forgive those who are guilty of sin;
you don't look at the sins of your people who are left alive.
You will not stay angry forever, because you enjoy being kind.
MICAH 7:18, NCV

us back to himself through Christ.... no longer counting people's sins against them" (NLT).

No More Yardstick

I don't think we can begin to imagine how radical Christ's New Testament message of grace sounded to a people who had been living under the Law for thousands of years. The thought that there might be a different way to approach God—a better way—was appealing to some Jews but threatening to many others.

For those who kept stumbling over the rules and regulations set up by the religious elite—never quite measuring up to the yardstick of the Law—the idea that God might love them apart from what they did must have been incredibly liberating.

But for the Jewish hierarchy who had mastered the Law and felt quite proud of it, Jesus's words surely posed a threat. His message pierced their religious facades, revealing the darkness of their hearts and, quite frankly, making them mad. Rather than running to the grace and forgiveness He offered, they kept defaulting to the yardstick—using it to justify themselves one minute, wielding it as a weapon against Jesus the next.*

"You come from Nazareth?" they said, pointing the yardstick. "Nothing good comes from Nazareth." *That's one whack for you.* "You eat with tax collectors and sinners? That's even worse." *Whack, whack.* "You heal on the Sabbath?" they screamed, waving their rules and regulations. *Off with Your head!*

The Sadducees and Pharisees had no room in their religion for freedom. As a result, they had no room for Christ. They were people of the yardstick. Even though Jesus kept insisting He hadn't come to "abolish the Law or the Prophets...but to fulfill them" (Matthew 5:17), they just wouldn't listen. Like little children they plugged their ears and kept singing the same old tune, though a New Song had been sent from heaven.

---

* Please let me tell you how much I love the nation of Israel. I fully believe they are the chosen people of God and a precious family into which I have been adopted. When I speak of the spiritual pride and blindness of the religious hierarchy of Jesus's day, it is not to condemn the Jews. Instead, I see my own tendency—and the tendency of the body of Christ today—to fall into spiritual pride and blindness when we love our "form of godliness" but miss "the power thereof" (2 Timothy 3:5, KJV).

Which is so very sad. Especially when you consider that the very Law they were so zealous for had been intended to *prepare* them for the Messiah rather than *keep* them from acknowledging Him.

After all, God established His original covenant with Abraham long before He gave Moses the Law—430 years before, to be exact (Galatians 3:17). The love the Father extended to Abraham and to all those who came after him had no strings attached. It was based on the recipient's acceptance of grace from beginning to end.

But somehow Israel fell in love with the Law rather than in love with their God. And we are in danger of doing the same thing. Exalting rules as the pathway to heaven. Embracing formulas as our salvation. Worshiping our own willpower rather than allowing the power of God to work in us to transform our lives.[5]

Such self-induced holiness didn't work for the Jews, and it doesn't work for us. That's why Jesus had to come.

The Law had originally been given "to show people their sins," Galatians 3:19 tells us. But it was "designed to last only until the coming of the child who was promised" (NLT). Though the yardstick of the Law helped keep us in line, it was never intended to save us. Only Christ could do that. And oh may I tell you how that comforts my soul?

I'll never forget the day I handed Jesus my yardstick. I had been saved since childhood, but I was almost thirty before the message of grace finally made the trip from my head to my heart, setting me "free from the law of sin and death" (Romans 8:2). As the light of the good news finally penetrated the darkness of my self-condemning mind, the "perfect love" 1 John 4:18 speaks of finally drove out my insecurity, which had always been rooted in fear of punishment.

When I finally laid down my Pharisee pride and admitted that in myself I would never be—could never be—enough, I experienced a breakthrough that has radically changed my life. For as I surrendered my yardstick—the tool of comparison that had caused so much mental torment and a sense of separation from God—Jesus took it from my hands. Then, with a look of great love, He broke it over His knee and turned it into a cross, reminding me that He died so I wouldn't have to.

That the punishment I so fully deserve has already been paid for.

That the way has been made for everyone who will believe in Jesus not only to come to Him but to come back home to the heart of God.

A Place to Lay Our Hearts

From the moment God so kindly exploded the concept of this book in my soul, I've had just one prayer. It is the prayer Paul prayed for all believers in Ephesians 3:17–19:

> And I pray that you, being rooted and established in love, may have power,
> together with all the saints, to grasp how wide and long and high and deep is
> the love of Christ, and to know this love that surpasses knowledge—that you
> may be filled to the measure of all the fullness of God.

I believe that everything we were made for and everything we've ever wanted is found in these three little verses. But in order to appropriate the all-encompassing love of God, we must give up our obsession with formulas and yardsticks. But how do we do that? Paul's prayer reveals an important key: "that you...may have power... to *know* this love that surpasses knowledge" (emphasis added).

The marvelous incongruity of that statement hit me several years ago. "Wait, Lord! How can I know something that surpasses knowledge?" I asked.

His answer came sweet and low to my spirit. *You have to stop trying to understand it and start accepting it, Joanna. Just let Me love you.*

For the reality is, no matter how hard we try, we will never be able to explain or deserve such amazing grace and incredible love. Nor can we escape it.

It's just too *wide,* Ephesians 3:18 tells us. We can't get around it.

It's just too *high.* We can't get over it.

It's so *long* we'll never be able to outrun it.

And it's so *deep* we'll never be able to exhaust it.

Bottom line: You can't get away from God's love no matter how hard you try. Because He's pursuing you, my friend. Maybe it's time to stop running away from love and start running toward it.

Even if, at times, it seems too good to be true.

CHOOSING LOVE

I don't know why Jesus chose me to love. Really, I don't. Perhaps you don't understand why He chose you. But He did. Really, He did. Until we get around to accepting His amazing, undeserved favor, I fear we will miss everything a relationship with Christ really means.

When my husband proposed to me so many years ago, I didn't say, "Wait a minute, John. Do you have any idea what you're getting into?" I didn't pull out a list of reasons why he couldn't possibly love me or a rap sheet detailing my inadequacies to prove why he shouldn't—although there were and are many.

No way! I just threw my arms open wide and accepted his love. I would have been a fool to turn down an offer like that.

I wonder what would happen in our lives if we stopped resisting God's love and started receiving it. What if we stopped trying to do the math, stopped striving to earn His favor? What if we just accepted the altogether-too-good-to-be-true news that the yardstick has been broken and the Cross has opened a door to intimacy with our Maker?

For if we are ever to be His beloved, we must be willing to *be* loved.

Simple, huh? And yet oh so hard. Like my friend Lisa, many of us are plagued by love-doubt. We have hidden tombs yet to be opened. Dark secrets that keep us hanging back. Soul-sicknesses that have left us crippled and embittered by our inability to forgive or forget. Graveclothes that keep tripping us up and fears that hold us back from believing the good news could ever be true for people like us.

I wonder...

Maybe it's time to look in the mirror and start witnessing to ourselves.

Maybe it's time we stop living by what we feel and start proclaiming what our spirits already know: "I have been chosen by God. Whether I feel loved or believe I deserve it, from this moment on I choose to be loved."

Say it out loud: "I choose to be loved."

You may have to force yourself to say the words. Today your emotions may not correspond with what you've just declared. It is likely you may have to repeat the same words tomorrow. And do it again the next day. And the next.

But I promise that as you start appropriating what God has already declared as truth, something's going to shift in the heavenly regions. More important, something's going to shift in you.

So say those words as many times as you need to...until the message gets through your thick head to your newly tender heart. Until you finally come to believe what's been true all along.

Shh...listen. Do you hear it?

It's Love.

And He's calling your name.

So the sisters sent word to Jesus,
"Lord, the one you love is sick."
When he heard this, Jesus said,
"This sickness will not end in death.
No, it is for God's glory so that
God's Son may be glorified through it."
Jesus loved Martha and her sister and Lazarus.
Yet when he heard that Lazarus was sick,
he stayed where he was two more days.
Then he said to his disciples, "Let us go back to Judea."....
After he had said this, he went on to tell them,
"Our friend Lazarus has fallen asleep;
but I am going there to wake him up."

JOHN 11:3–7, 11

Lord, the One You Love Is Sick

The message was brief, but as Jesus listened, He must have felt the pain behind the words. His friend Lazarus was sick.

Breathless in his hurry and dusty from the journey, a weary messenger waited before Him. The disciples waited as well. What would Jesus say? More to the point, what would Jesus do? They'd seen amazing things in the years they'd traveled with the man from Galilee. The lame walked. The blind could see. Even lepers were made completely whole. Surely Jesus would act quickly on behalf of this man who was no stranger.

But they were twenty miles from Bethany, across the River Jordan from the land of Judea—a hard day's journey from the family Jesus loved. There were enemies in nearby Jerusalem to consider, even rumors of a death warrant. Still, knowing how Jesus felt about Lazarus, the disciples must have readied themselves to leave immediately. Then Jesus broke the silence with what surely sounded to their ears like incredibly good news.

"This sickness will not end in death," He declared to the men standing around Him. "No, it is for God's glory so that God's Son may be glorified through it" (John 11:4).

It was good news indeed—especially to the messenger, who hurried back to tell the waiting sisters. What a relief to be able to say that their brother wouldn't die. That Jesus would come and all would be well.

But little did the man know that when he arrived back in Bethany, he'd find two grief-stricken sisters and Jesus's friend Lazarus already dead and gone.[1]

WHEN LIFE DOESN'T MAKE SENSE

It wasn't supposed to be this way. Death, grief, and pain were not part of God's original plan. We were created for life, for an eternity of close communion with our Maker. We were not meant to suffer sickness or feel grief's inexplicable loss.

You and I were made for paradise.

But according to Genesis, the arrival of sin changed all that. Adam and Eve's rebellion opened a dark door, and death entered the world like a conqueror, sweeping indiscriminately across humanity. Turning one person against another, striking down one with illness and another with hatred. Sin has spent millenniums ravaging homes and hearts, leaving a trail of brokenness, tears, and sorrow.

Yet of all sin's evil residue, perhaps nothing torments us more than the questions that swirl in our minds.

Why?

Why am I sick?

Why is my marriage broken?

Why can't I find someone to love?

Why did my friend have to die?

I'm sure Martha and Mary struggled with questions as well. Could they have done something more? Perhaps they should have sent word to Jesus as soon as Lazarus's symptoms worsened. Perhaps they should have been more forceful in the wording of their message. It was a little vague, after all: "Lord, the one you love is sick" (John 11:3). Perhaps their friend hadn't understood how serious the situation had become.

But lingering somewhere in their minds, as they do in ours at times like these, two terrible queries must have wrestled for prominence:

Maybe this is punishment for something we've done. Maybe it's our fault our brother died.

Or perhaps, and even more painful to contemplate:

Maybe Jesus doesn't love us as much as we love Him.

MAKING SENSE OF SENSELESS THINGS

We humans are big on formulas. We need things to add up, so we're always coming up with rationales and reasons for the way the world works. And it's important that we do, for such curiosity helps make sense of things around us, opening doors to discoveries and innovations that would not be made without it.

But, unfortunately, our insistence that life should always add up often results in faulty conclusions. Especially when we're attempting to reconcile the problem of pain and suffering with belief in a loving, caring God.

One of the most damaging misperceptions of many Christians is that if we are walking with God, nothing bad should ever happen to us. While we might not admit it or even see it, "Bless me, bless me" has been much of the church's cry and expectation these past few decades. So much so that I'm afraid we've actually fallen for the lie that a life of ease and obvious blessing is always an indication of God's favor.

If good things are happening to you, it is because you're doing something right. If you're walking through difficulties, it is because you're doing something wrong.

Sounds logical to our human minds. And it sounded good to the people of the Bible as well. When faced with Job's suffering, his friends insisted there had to be a reason for the painful boils, the destruction of his home, and the devastating loss of his family. "Come on, Job," they prodded. "Fess up! You've obviously done something wrong."

We see the same mind-set in the New Testament, for the scribes and Pharisees loved formulas as well. They had created an encyclopedia-sized index of rules and guidelines for gaining God's pleasure and, thus, His goodies. They, too, were prone to believe that an absence of certain goodies indicated an absence of God's pleasure. If for some reason you fell ill, they reasoned only one thing could explain it: either you or your parents had sinned, and thus you deserved your current state.[2]

It's no wonder that in Jesus's day the lame and the leper, the blind and the deaf were relegated to being outcasts and beggars. Because they deserved their fate, the only responsibility society felt was an occasional gift, a couple of alms, as they passed them begging on the streets.

It was a neat and tidy system…unless, of course, you happened to be one of those sick or maimed or afflicted. Someone like Lazarus.

Sick and Tired of Being Sick and Tired

When we're told that Mary and Martha sent word their brother was ill, the Bible uses the Greek word *astheneo*. According to one writer, "This isn't just the word for a virus or flu bug, it was used for a prolonged illness. Lazarus was 'feeble with sickness'. It is the word used of impotence—lack of power—an ongoing illness or weakness."[3]

My friend Renee knows a little of what Lazarus may have gone through. Medication she took many years ago severely damaged her heart, lungs, and nerves, and they continue to deteriorate. Many days Renee is confined to her bed. On a good morning taking a shower requires an hour and leaves her breathless. My friend is doing the best she can—eating right, trying to exercise. However, doctors can do little except treat the symptoms. Unless Jesus intervenes, my friend may die from her disease.

But you would never know it when meeting her. Renee is one of the most vibrant and joyful people I've ever met—sunshine with glasses on. Her conversation rarely circles around any well-deserved health complaint. Instead, when I answer her phone calls, I am greeted with, "Joanna Gloria! How are you today?"

I love that girl! She is a gift to me and to the body of Christ.

Renee gives thanks to God for every day. For each breath. For the life she has. Yet while I marvel at her endurance and especially at the peaceful joy that literally surrounds her, I must confess I sometimes wonder why. Why Renee? Why not someone who actually deserves a painful death sentence such as this?

But then, I suppose that could very well involve me.

For none of us deserves health. None of us deserves this miraculous gift of life. It's all grace, every bit of it. Even the hard parts. Even the parts we don't understand.

I don't believe Lazarus was ill because of sin in his life. And neither is my friend Renee.

Life just isn't as cut-and-dried as many of us want to make it. We can't point at a particular trouble and assign blame. There's too much we can't see and don't understand.

But let me be clear. Just as it would be wrong to assume that all sickness is caused by some failure on the ill person's part, it would also be incorrect to say that sin has no consequences. Or that sickness never has its roots in disobedience.

After healing a paralyzed man by the pool called Bethesda, Jesus later went out of His way to find the man in the temple. "See, you are well again," Jesus told him. "Stop sinning or something worse may happen to you" (John 5:14).

For there is a disease much more damaging to humanity than those commonly diagnosed by doctors. And Jesus knew that. It is the curse that has plagued our hearts from the moment Eve's lips touched the forbidden fruit.

The very sickness He came to cure.

FALLEN ILL

Of all the ailments in all the world, no illness has caused as much pain or as much destruction to us humans as the widespread but often misdiagnosed inner plague called *S-I-N*.

In these three little letters, we find the DNA of a supervirus that has destroyed more careers, more marriages, more families, more churches, and more men, women, boys, and girls than all of earth's diseases put together. It has shredded more reputations, shattered more hearts, and destroyed more minds than any pandemic.

Try as we might, we can't get away from it, for it is interwoven in the fabric of our humanity. Passed down through generation after generation of both good men and bad, gentle mothers and raging lunatics, noble kings and evil tyrants. It rests inside me, and it abides in you as well. For it might be said of each of us, "Lord, the one you love is sick."

We might not be ax murderers. Yet the slander that slips so easily off our tongues murders more than we know.

We might not be meth addicts breaking into houses and terrorizing old ladies to get enough money for another high. But our escapist thinking can be just as dangerous—eroding our marriages and our homes, causing us to be physically present in our relationships yet emotionally unavailable.

We might not be scam artists or child abusers, prostitutes or thugs, but the envy and lust and anger and pride that lurk inside us trouble the heart of God just as much as any of our darker pastimes.

Because sin—all sin—destroys. It maims, and it cuts us off from the life we need.

And if we're honest with ourselves, we know it. We feel it. We are, every one of us, sin-sick—there is no other way to describe it. And our transgressions, if not confessed and dealt with, separate us from God, causing the love-doubt that haunts our nights and clouds our days.

But we don't have to live that way. Because if we'll simply agree with the diagnosis, Jesus has already provided the cure.

Forever Searching—Forever Found

Ten years ago while writing *Having a Mary Heart in a Martha World,* I had a strange recurring dream. At least once a week, I would dream of waking in a dark bedroom

---

What God Does with Our Sins

Rosalind Goforth, a well-known missionary to China, struggled many years with an oppressive burden of guilt and sin that left her feeling like a spiritual failure. Finally, out of desperation, she sat down with her Bible and a concordance, determined to find out how God views the faults of His children. At the top of the paper, she wrote these words: "What God Does with Our Sins." Then she searched the Scriptures, compiling this list of seventeen truths:

1. He lays them on His Son—Jesus Christ (Isaiah 53:6).
2. Christ takes them away (John 1:29).
3. They are removed an immeasurable distance—as far as east is from west (Psalm 103:12).
4. When sought for [they] are not found (Jeremiah 50:20).
5. The Lord forgives them (1 John 1:9; Ephesians 1:7; Psalm 103:3).
6. He cleanses them all away by the blood of His Son (1 John 1:7).
7. He cleanses them as white as snow or wool (Isaiah 1:18; Psalm 51:7).

in a strange yet somewhat familiar house. In my dream I'd wander through a maze of hallways and rooms looking for something I'd lost. Groping in the dark, I'd inch my way through endless corridors.

The frustration of the search was surpassed only by the urgency I felt. I had to find it—whatever "it" was. But I never did, no matter how many times I had the dream or how diligently I searched. When I'd waken, the intensity of the dream would follow me throughout the day. It felt so real I'd find myself making a mental note to go to that house (wherever it was) and find the treasure I'd somehow misplaced.

Odd dream. And one I didn't fully understand until nearly a year after that first book was published. The illumination finally came in the form of a letter from a reader, a representative of a ministry that we had asked to consider recommending the book.

---

   8. He abundantly pardons them (Isaiah 55:7).

   9. He tramples them underfoot (Micah 7:19).

10. He remembers them no more (Hebrews 10:17; Ezekiel 33:16).

11. He casts them behind His back (Isaiah 38:17).

12. He casts them into the depths of the sea (Micah 7:19).

13. He will not impute [or charge] us with sins (Romans 4:8).

14. He covers them (Romans 4:7).

15. He blots them out (Isaiah 43:25).

16. He blots them out [like] a thick cloud (Isaiah 44:22).

17. He blots out even the proof against us, nailing it to His Son's cross (Colossians 2:14).[4]

Blessed is he whose transgressions are forgiven,

whose sins are covered.

PSALM 32:1

The letter writer was very kind in her comments about the book, but she informed me gently that the ministry she represented would be unable to carry the title on their book tables. Their policy required all recommended books to include a clear plan of salvation. And mine, while written well for established Christians, had not done that.

"You see, Joanna," she wrote, "I was forty-two years old before I was told I could have a personal relationship with Christ. Though I'd gone to church since I was a child, no one had told me how to accept Jesus as my own personal Savior. That's why it's so important to tell people that simply believing in God isn't enough—we must accept the gift Christ offers."

And she was right. The Bible clearly teaches that belief in God's existence doesn't save our souls. "Even the demons believe—and tremble!" (James 2:19, NKJV). If we are ever to find the intimate and personal relationship God longs to have with us, there is only one way. One truth and one life (John 14:6).

You see, the treasure I'd searched for in my dream is found in only one place: in the Person of the God-Man, Jesus Christ. He is much more than an *anecdote*—a heartwarming story portraying a spiritual truth. He is the *antidote* to the poison of sin and the singular cure for the sin-sickness that has infected humanity since that fateful day in the garden.

For only Jesus can provide a Lazarus awakening for the soul-sleep that plagues us all.

AWAKE, SLEEPER!

Two days had passed since they'd heard about Lazarus's sickness. The disciples must have wondered why Jesus waited so long to go to Bethany or if He would go at all. There were plenty of reasons not to, including a death warrant. But then the Master gathered them and said, "Let us go back to Judea" (John 11:7).

The disciples tried to dissuade Him, bringing up the religious mob that had attempted to stone Him just weeks before. But Jesus was unmoved by their argument, telling them, "Our friend Lazarus has fallen asleep; but I am going there to wake him up" (John 11:11).

Stop a moment and reread that last sentence.

"He has fallen asleep, but I'm going to *wake him up.*" Oh how those words speak to me.

Throughout the Bible sleep is synonymous with death. Ironically, as with Snow White, a poisoned fruit caused Adam and Eve to fall into a spiritual unconsciousness that still affects you and me today. When God told the first couple not to eat from the forbidden tree, when He said, "You will surely die" (Genesis 2:17), He wasn't kidding. The moment they disobeyed, the center of their beings fell asleep.

The Invitation

There is no more important question than the one asked by a Philippian jailer over two thousand years ago: "What must I do to be saved?" (Acts 16:30).

Jesus answered that question once and for all by taking the punishment for our sins upon Himself. We simply have to accept the free gift of salvation He offers. How do we do that? The Billy Graham Evangelistic Association outlines four steps for receiving Christ:

- Admit your need. (I am a sinner.)
- Be willing to turn from your sins (repent).
- Believe that Jesus Christ died for you on the cross and rose from the grave.
- Pray a prayer like this: Dear Lord Jesus, I know that I am a sinner, and I ask for Your forgiveness. I believe You died for my sins and rose from the dead. I turn from my sins and invite You to come into my heart and life. I want to trust and follow You as my Lord and Savior. In Your Name, amen.[5]

Yet to all who received him, to those who believed in his name,
he gave the right to become children of God.

JOHN 1:12

The part of them that had communed best with their Creator—that is, their spirits—died.[6]

Likewise, our spirits remain locked in death-sleep until we meet Jesus Christ as our personal Savior. Until the Prince of Peace wakens our slumbering hearts with a tender kiss and the sprinkling of His shed blood, the most important part of our beings will remain lifeless and dead. Only Christ can perform the spiritual CPR we so desperately need.

But it's important to realize that even after we commit our lives to Jesus, the danger of spiritual slumber is never far away. Even though we are no longer dead in our spirits, it's still possible for us to be lulled back to sleep in our souls. Suffering from a type of spiritual narcolepsy and sleepwalking through life, we remain loved by Jesus—just as Lazarus was—but in desperate need of being awakened by an encounter with the living God.

How is it possible that Christians could fall into such slumber? In most cases it doesn't happen suddenly. Nodding off to the things of God is usually an incremental process. A slow numbing of the heart, along with a diminished ability to hear the Spirit's voice. A drifting and dreaming of our souls as they follow other pursuits.

In my case such seemingly innocent naps have often started with a lullaby. A compromising tune hummed by the Deceiver one day. A long ballad of self-pity sung by Satan the next. To think that Lucifer might use his unholy hymns to soothe us into spiritual oblivion makes sense to me. After all, he seems to have quite a musical repertoire.

It's no big deal, he serenaded King David as the man after God's own heart began to chase after another man's wife (2 Samuel 11:2–4).

Everyone's doing it, he hummed softly to Samson as he lured the strongest man who ever lived to trade the secret of his strength for another night in the arms of a Philistine beauty (Judges 16:15–17).

Nobody cares about you, he crooned to a tired prophet as Elijah sat under a broom tree of discouragement (1 Kings 19:3–4).

Satanic songs every one of them, and there are as many different lyrics as there are listening ears. Music to make us doubt God's love. Tunes to make us cease to care. Lullabies intended to lull us bye-bye to the point where we're blind to the Enemy's devices and deaf to the Spirit's voice.

Fast asleep. Drifting farther away from the God we serve and the love we need. And deeply, desperately in need of waking up.

Years ago I was staying at a hotel in Houston, Texas. When I called the front desk to schedule a wake-up call, they promised to do just that and more.

"If you don't answer the phone, we'll knock at the door," the man on the line said. "If you don't answer the door, we will come in and shake you until you get up."

Now that's what I call service! A bit unsettling but, still, service!

I believe God would love to do the same for us if we'd just give Him permission. He knows how easily we sleep through spiritual alarm clocks. He's watched us consistently shrug off His stirrings when He's tried to revive us. But our heavenly Father is willing to go through all that and more if we will only listen and respond to Him.

We're asleep, Lord Jesus. Wake us up! should be our daily prayer. *Wake us up to Your loving mercy. Wake us up to Your goodness and Your power to save.* Even though, like Mary and Martha, we sometimes wonder, *Maybe this sickness is punishment for my sins.* Or, *Maybe Jesus doesn't love me as much as I love Him.*

Wake us up, Lord Jesus, to the thorough trustworthiness of Your ways, for only You can take what was meant for evil and turn it into good (Genesis 50:20).

OUR GREAT REDEEMER

Of all the titles of Jesus, I've come to appreciate most that He is my Redeemer. After walking so many years with the Lord, through both good times and bad, I can declare along with Job, "I know that my Redeemer lives" (Job 19:25). For He takes the worthless and makes it precious when we trust His loving hands.

When God interrupted humanity's downward spiral by sending His own Son, Jesus came into a culture that expected the Messiah to set up a kingdom free from problems, sorrow, and pain. Even His own disciples expected He would topple Rome and set up a new regime complete with corner offices and special perks reserved just for them.

Those looking forward to the Promised One had always believed He would reinvent the world.

Instead, God chose to redeem it.

Which means sin is still present and Satan is still active. Murder and violent wars cover the earth. Sickness ravages bodies and minds and hearts. Too often the innocent die young. Surely, we think, there has to be a better way.

After all, God could have pushed the reset button long ago, at the beginning of time. He could have taken one look at the mess we humans had made—our rebellion, our hatred, our immorality and idolatry—and decided to delete it all. With one push of a button, God could have rebooted and started over.

Instead, He became a man. And on the cross He took the weight of our mistakes. All my failures, all your hurts, all our devastation. With a final breath He redeemed it all.

"It is finished," Jesus said just before He died (John 19:30). And it was. For with those words came the great exchange. His death became ours so that our lives could become His. And three days later tragedy turned into triumph as the Lamb came bursting forth from the tomb like a Lion. Silencing hell's laughter, Jesus snatched the keys of death and the grave and shattered Satan's schemes, redeeming you and me and causing all the destruction the Enemy had perpetrated against us to boomerang back on his deceiving, thieving, troublemaking head.

Christ still does the same recycling work today, taking the garbage of people's lives and fashioning masterpieces of grace. Reclaiming prostitutes and murderers, lepers and beggars, greedy executives and desperate housewives and transforming them all into life-size trophies of His love.

This is the power of the gospel. This is the centerpiece of the good news!

"Christ did not come to make bad men good," Ravi Zacharias points out, "but to make dead men alive."[7] For our heavenly Father knew we needed more than a renovation. We needed a resurrection. And that's what Jesus came to bring.

"This sickness will not end in death," Jesus reassured the disciples in John 11:4, and He whispers the same hope to you and me today.

Go ahead and fill in the blank with your situation. "Lord, the one you love is _____." Diagnosed with cancer, facing bankruptcy, losing a marriage—the list can go on and on. But not one of those problems is too big for God.

This sickness, this heartache, this life-altering situation will not end in death, Jesus promises. Instead, if we'll respond to His invitation and leave the tombs of our sin and even our doubt, our lives will declare the truth of His next statement: "It is for God's glory."

Because, as Saint Irenaeus once said, "The glory of God is man fully alive."[8]

So cure my spiritual narcolepsy, Lord. Rouse me from my slumber. Shake me, if necessary, until I respond. But whatever You do, dear Jesus, don't leave me the same.

For good things come to those who wake!

Then he said to his disciples, "Let us go to back to Judea.".…
After he had said this, he went on to tell them,
"Our friend Lazarus has fallen asleep."

JOHN 11:7, 11

Our Friend Lazarus

A h, the indescribable joy of being loved!
I am currently in the enviable position of having two men absolutely gaga over me.

The first one, my wonderful husband, isn't quite as enthusiastic as the second, though John shows me love a hundred ways every day. But the second guy—well, this little Romeo can't seem to do enough to show how much he adores me. His attentions come complete with dandelions and stick-figure cards…and lots and lots of verbal declarations.

It's not just the words that make my heart go pitter-patter, for I've been blessed to hear "I love you" many times throughout my life. What makes Josh's words so delicious is the *way* he says them. As though he really means them.

He doesn't throw them flippantly over his shoulder as he goes outside to play. Nor does he use his affection to win his own way. Not yet, anyway. For now, at least, his professions of love are just pure adoration. And lately, for whatever reason, Josh infuses these three syllables with such ardor and emotion they take my breath away.

"Mom," he says a bit solemnly, pausing a moment until he has my complete attention. Then, in a slow, sweet drawl marked by his speech impediment, he draws out the middle word to give it extra emphasis. "I wuuuuv you."

Suddenly all is right with my world. And more than right—it's wonderful. Joshua throws himself into my arms, and I return his love, holding him as if I could hold him forever.

Of course, after a bit—sometimes longer if I'm lucky—Josh disengages. He gives me an extra-big squeeze, and then with a jelly-smeared kiss, he hops off my lap and goes back to play.

But before he does, while we're still wrapped in each other's arms, my heart captures a snapshot with a scribbled caption describing the joy of being loved. Not for what I've done, not even for who I am. But simply because the mere sight of me causes such intense emotion that words are required—not just once but several times a day.

I know it's just a phase. I know Joshua will grow up and become enamored with much more than me. Oh, he'll still express his love—that's just the kind of guy he is—but he won't do it as often or as intensely. So for now I'm determined to enjoy every minute. Whenever Josh flings himself my way, I stop what I'm doing to drink in the treasured sweetness. There is an indescribable joy to being loved like that, and I don't want to miss it.

Why am I telling you this? To make you wish you'd had an unexpected pregnancy at age forty that resulted in an amazing little boy like mine?

No, though I could wish no greater gift for anyone.

I'm telling you this because Joshua is teaching me about the kind of relationship Christ longs to have with me. The love affair I'm enjoying with my six-year-old is the kind of love affair God wants to enjoy with all His children. The intermingling of hearts He has longed for since the foundation of the world.

The Loneliness of God

That God was lonely had never occurred to the angels. All powerful, all knowing, the eternal Beginning and eternal End, the three-in-one Godhead—how could the Almighty feel any lack?

And yet there'd been a quiet restlessness about Yahweh for some time. A far-off look now and then revealed a yearning, a longing. Almost a sadness. Perhaps, then, it wasn't such a surprise when the Uncreated declared His desire to create.

After witnessing five days of extraordinary work, watching God drop a small blue-green orb into created space, then fill it with one marvelous invention after another, the angels must have stood on tiptoe to see what God would do next.

"Let us make man in our image," said the Creator, stooping down to fill His hands with dust. With great care the Eternal One shaped His work. Then, bending over, He gently breathed into the lifeless clay, and a man was created...then a woman. The two were handsome enough, the angels thought, though a bit ordinary, especially when measured against all they'd seen. Yet God seemed quite pleased.

Perhaps, the angels pondered, this creation had some special talent they were unaware of, some unique quality that would make them useful to the kingdom. So they waited to see these humans perform.

But soon it became evident that all God's previous work—the soaring mountains, the lush green valleys, the glorious sunrises, and watercolor sunsets—had been made for the pleasure and delight of man and woman, His last created works.

But not just for their pleasure. It was for something else as well. The shimmering world, the angels soon realized, was simply a backdrop. A stage upon which they would watch creation's true purpose unfold.

For all of it had been made to facilitate God's passionate pursuit of relationship with humankind.

What We're Made For

Perhaps you've never considered how much your heavenly Father longs to know you and be known by you. We've been told that we were born with a God-shaped hole— a spiritual vacuum that can't be filled by anything or anyone except God Himself. But have you ever considered that God might have a *you*-shaped hole, an emptiness that only you can fill?

That's the overarching implication of the biblical message. From the book of Genesis to the Song of Solomon, from Ecclesiastes to Malachi, from Matthew to Revelation, the entire Bible records an epic story of the ever-reaching, always-pursuing, tenaciously tender love of God. I appreciate the way The Message expresses Ephesians 1:4–6:

Long before he laid down earth's foundations, [God] had us in mind, had settled on us as the focus of his love, to be made whole and holy by his love.

Long, long ago he decided to adopt us into his family through Jesus Christ. (What pleasure he took in planning this!) He wanted us to enter into the celebration of his lavish gift-giving by the hand of his beloved Son.

See what I mean? The Bible is clear. We have a God who is gaga about us.

The question is, are we gaga about Him?

I want to be head over heels in love with God, but the problem is I don't always know how to go about it. I'm learning a lot about gaga love from my little son, however, and I'm learning better how to love Jesus from a man in the Bible whose words aren't even recorded. While we don't have a lot of background information from which to speculate and no physical description of Lazarus, we still learn some important things about this man from Scripture.

First, Jesus loved Lazarus.

Second, that love translated into a close relationship between the two.

The first point may seem obvious and somewhat unimportant. After all, Jesus loves everyone. And yet the narrator of the biblical account highlights their closeness several times to make sure we know that this was not merely a generic acquaintance.

In John 11:3, for instance, Lazarus's sisters send word: "Lord, the one you *love* is sick."

Later, in verse 5, John reiterates: "Jesus *loved* Martha and her sister and Lazarus."

Even the Jews who later gathered at Lazarus's funeral must have been aware of an extra-special relationship between Christ and the man they mourned, for when they saw Jesus weeping at the tomb, they said, "See how he *loved* him!" (verse 36).

Jesus loved Lazarus. He loved Martha and Mary as well (verse 5). And I believe the three siblings reciprocated that love. Scripture tells us Christ returned often to Bethany. The family must have brought Him great joy and comfort, offering a home where He was welcomed with open arms, accepted, and truly beloved.

Hearing that Lazarus was ill must have grieved Jesus's heart, even though He knew how the story would end. When Jesus arrived in Bethany and saw Mary weeping, John 11:33 tells us "he was deeply moved in spirit and troubled." So troubled, in fact, that He may have literally groaned out loud. The Greek word for "deeply moved," *embrimaomai,* comes from the root word that means "to snort with anger; to have indignation."[1] Jesus didn't take the family's pain lightly. For Lazarus was much more than a follower.

When referring to Mary and Martha's brother, Jesus used a term that seems generic on the surface but is far more intimate than that—not to mention powerful. And it can change our relationship with our Maker if we will seek to be named by it as well.

When talking about Lazarus, Jesus called him "friend" (John 11:11).

FRIEND OF GOD

What does it mean to be a friend of God? I'm talking about an honest-to-goodness, true-blue, when-the-chips-are-down kind of friend of God.

I've felt the Lord challenging me with this very question. I'd like to think Jesus considers me a friend. But am I really? Am I someone He can feel safe with? Is my heart a place with plenty of room for Him to spread out and relax? Is *mi casa* truly His *casa*?

It isn't easy finding a friend like that. Just ask any Hollywood celebrity who is hounded by friends who seem sincere but are really out for what they can get.

In his book on the psychology of fame and the problems of celebrity, author David Giles describes the loneliness that often stalks famous people: "On meeting each new acquaintance, the question becomes not so much, 'Does this person like me for who I am?' but 'Does this person like me for *what* I am?' "[2]

According to Giles, even the Greek philosopher Cicero experienced this. Back in 60 BC he "complained that, despite the 'droves of friends' surrounding him, he was unable to find one with whom he could 'fetch a private sigh.' "[3]

I wonder if God ever feels like that. Does His heart hurt when He realizes most people hang around Him for what they can get?

For the contacts they can make.

For the warm fuzzies they feel.

For the benefits and perks that come with Christianity—peace, joy, provision.

Or for the rewards they expect when they offer God a calculated gift of service. Such a self-centered, results-oriented relationship must grieve the heart of the Almighty. It certainly causes us to miss out on the intimacy He intends.

Help Me Love You More!

In his book *Crazy Love*, Francis Chan invites us to invite God to help us love Him more.

> If you merely pretend that you enjoy God or love Him, He knows. You can't fool Him; don't even try.
>
> Instead, tell Him how you feel. Tell Him that He isn't the most important thing in this life to you, and that you're sorry for that. Tell Him that you've been lukewarm, that you've chosen _____ over Him time and again. Tell Him that you want Him to change you, that you long to genuinely enjoy Him. Tell Him how you want to experience true satisfaction and pleasure and joy in your relationship with Him. Tell Him you want to love Him more than anything on this earth. Tell Him you want to treasure the kingdom of heaven so much that you'd willingly sell everything in order to get it. Tell Him what you like about Him, what you appreciate, and what brings you joy.
>
> *Jesus, I need to give myself up. I am not strong enough to love You and walk with You on my own. I can't do it, and I need You. I need You deeply and desperately. I believe You are worth it, that You are better than anything else I could have in this life or the next. I want You. And when I don't, I want to want You. Be all in me. Take all of me. Have Your way with me.*[4]

> *My heart says of you, "Seek his face!"*
> *Your face, LORD, I will seek.*
> PSALM 27:8

In *The Divine Romance,* an imaginative retelling of the biblical story of Exodus, Gene Edwards paints a poignant picture of God's heart toward us. One scene in particular stands out in my mind. It depicts God watching as the people brought out of Egypt's bondage vow to serve Him always. Promising to obey Yahweh in everything both big and small, they bring all their treasures and fall on their faces to worship. And yet, as God looks on, "unobserved by all," He is struck by a "deep sadness." Edwards writes:

A long, deep groan of sorrow, unheard by human ears but shattering the tranquility of the entire heavenly host, rose up from his depths.

> *I did not require of you*
> *your wealth nor coins of gold.*
> *What need have I of these?*
> *I did not ask of you*
> *that you serve me.*
> *Do I, the Mighty One,*
> *need to be waited upon?*
> *Neither did I ask of you*
> *your worship nor your prayers*
> *nor even your obedience.*

He paused. Once more a long, mournful groan rose from his breast.

> *I have asked but this of you,*
> *that you love me...*
> *love me...*
> *love me.*[5]

God's Love Language

I don't believe any of us intend to set aside a true relationship with God in favor of some kind of performance—whether it be practical or even spiritual. The tendency to do so, however, seems hard-wired in the fallen part of our nature. It's as though back in Eden a faulty switch was thrown, replacing the gift of relationship with the curse of works. Which, I suppose, is exactly what happened that long-ago day.

"Because you...ate from the tree about which I commanded you, 'You must not eat of it,' " God told the first humans, "cursed is the ground because of you; through painful toil you will eat of it all the days of your life" (Genesis 3:17).

From the moment Adam and Eve disobeyed God, the couple would have to work for their food. But please note: God never required them to work up a plan to restore their relationship with Him. For that labor had already begun, and it was God's work alone.

"The cross was no accident," Max Lucado writes in his beautiful book *God Came Near*. "...The moment the forbidden fruit touched the lips of Eve, the shadow of a cross appeared on the horizon."[6]

The brilliant plan of redemption was set in motion the moment sin entered the world. And all of it was orchestrated by God. A living, vibrant relationship with our Father was never intended to be the work of our hands no matter how noble our efforts might be.

Gene Edwards's story haunts me. *"I did not ask of you that you serve me,"* God cries out to His beloved. *"Neither did I ask of you your worship nor your prayers."*

Those are powerful statements, because they zero in on the two ways we Christians usually try to get close to God. Through service and through worship, the same methods by which Lazarus's sisters tended to relate to Jesus.

Martha, of course, is the poster child for service—the original Martha Stewart of Israel. Her story in Luke 10:38–42 highlights the difficulties that arise when we get so caught up in good works that we lose sight of our relationship with God. It's easy to become so enamored with the human approval that comes from giving our lives away—volunteering for worthy causes, teaching Sunday school every week, delivering meals to shut-ins, and so on—that we never get around to resting in God's presence, drinking in His life, and pouring out our love.

Though our acts of service are vital to our walk with God and even prove our faith, according to James 2:17, they were meant to be the outflow of a relationship with God—not a replacement for it.

Edwards's story reminds me that while God has chosen to involve us in His work of redeeming the world, He didn't really *need* to do that. In reality, all He had to do was speak—for He is the all-powerful One. Whatever was needed He could have done.

God didn't need us. But oh how He *wanted* us to be His own.

That's the freedom Jesus offered Martha. Freedom from the God she thought He was, forever demanding more, always more, and of a higher quality, always higher. In Christ she found a God who wanted to share her life, not consume it. A Father who wanted her love more than He wanted her busy service.

But what about worship? After all, that's what Mary seemed to offer Jesus, and He commended her for it. Could it be possible that God desires something more from us than that?

Before we delve into that question, it's important to note that Mary knew what true worship was. She knew it had far more to do with nurturing a relationship than coming up with the appropriate response to a message or singing the right combination of praise songs and hymns. She knew Jesus wanted her heart far more than her liturgy, as beautiful as it might be. He wanted to make her His own. That's why she was able to stop striving and simply sit at His feet. Her availability was more precious than any outward form of worship.

I realize it's almost sacrilegious in some areas of today's Christian culture to suggest that God might be looking for more than our praise. We've elevated worship to a place that nearly teeters on idolatry. We've said worship is our highest calling—and important it is.

But listen! The angels already provide God with praise. They surround the throne of God 24/7. You and I were not created to add voices to the angelic choir. We were created to enjoy an intimate relationship with the King of the Universe.

Please know how much I love praising God, how much I need it! There is something beautiful and profound about expressing my love for God through words and song. There is something sacred about lifting my hands, joining my voice with yours, and exalting Jesus with my lips. I can't live without it!

But if that is where my relationship with Jesus ends, I am missing it. Really missing it. Because it is possible to become addicted to praise without really becoming addicted to God. And when that happens, our worship ceases to be worship and turns into just another ritual. Moving and melodic perhaps, but in the end just empty religious words and motions.

Bottom line: If I truly want to be a friend of God, it won't be my service or my praise that brings Him joy. Instead, the kind of relationship I believe Christ longs for most may be exemplified best in the sibling who said and did the least.

In the beautiful acceptance Jesus offered Lazarus and the love Lazarus returned, we discover the good news of the gospel. Freedom from the tyranny of works and the spiritual contortions we often use in an attempt to please and/or appease our God. In the story of Lazarus, we are invited to relax. To simply enjoy hanging out with God.

Because Jesus isn't looking for servants.

He isn't looking for worshiping admirers.

He is looking for friends.

And the more unlikely the friendship, it seems, the better.

Groupies or Friends?

From the world's point of view, Jesus didn't seem very picky about His friendships. He hung out with the lowliest of the low—the despised, the forgotten, and the unnoticed. One of the accusations leveled against our Savior was that He was "a friend of tax collectors and 'sinners' " (Luke 7:34).

For the most part, that accusation was true. Jesus seemed far more interested in the sincerity of a heart than the perfection of a life, and He found many sincere seekers among those the religious elite labeled as "sinners." But it wasn't just the poor and the messed-up that Jesus came to save. He came for ordinary folks and the extraordinary as well.

"To all who received him," John proclaims in his gospel, "to those who believed in his name, he gave the right to become children of God" (John 1:12). You didn't have to perform or measure up to some religious standard to be Jesus's friend. You simply had to accept what He had to offer. However, the depth and type of friendship depended completely on the response of the person to whom it was offered. And it still does today.

As I was praying about this chapter and what the Holy Spirit wanted to say through it, one thing became very clear to me. Surrounded by people who claim His name, Christ still longs for a genuine friend. A real, true-blue, when-the-chips-are-down kind of friend. A friend who cares about what He cares about. A friend who looks to bring joy and comfort to His heart, with no strings attached. No hidden agendas. No secret wish lists.

Interestingly, in the Greek language there are two distinct words for "friend"— *philos* and *hetairos*. It is unfortunate that the English translation for both terms is the same word, for the Greek terms could not be more different.

The first word, *philos,* is the term Jesus used when He called Lazarus "our friend" in John 11:11. It denotes someone "loved, dear, befriended." It is an intimate classification reserved for those close to the heart.

The second term used in the Greek, *hetairos,* can be translated "comrade or companion," but it refers to a darker kind of relationship. According to Spiros Zodhiates,

> *hetaíros* refer[s] to comrades or companions who were mostly followers of a
> chief. They were not necessarily companions for the sake of helping the chief,
> but for getting whatever advantage they could.… The verb *hetaíré* basically
> means to keep company with or to establish and maintain a meretricious,
> pretentious, ostentatious, deceptive, and misleading friendship.[7]

Sounds a little like our society today, doesn't it? We are encouraged to network, schmooze, and work the angles. Do whatever it takes to succeed, we're told. Be friendly on the surface. Just make sure it furthers your agenda underneath.

"True friendship," on the other hand, as Zodhiates explains, "is expressed by the verb *phileo*…which means to appropriate another person's interests unselfishly."[8]

At its most benign, *hetairos* was used to describe the pupils or disciples of teachers or rabbis. But this wasn't the term Jesus used when speaking of His own disciples in John 15:15 (or anywhere else for that matter). "I no longer call you servants," Jesus told them, "because a servant does not know his master's business. Instead, I have called you friends [*philous*[9]], for everything that I learned from my Father I have made known to you."

Jesus wasn't fostering an arm's-length business relationship with those who followed Him. He sought a sweet communion that would make the disciples actual partakers of the divine nature (2 Peter 1:4, NKJV). Jesus promised to take everything God had given Him—the wisdom, the authority, the very character of God—and share it freely with them. What an incredible gift. What an unimaginable opportunity.

But not everyone appreciated the Lord's generosity. At least one of the disciples wanted what *he* wanted—human recognition, power, position.

When Judas betrayed Jesus in Gethsemane, hoping to force the Son of God to

---

What Kind of Friend Am I?

We've all had needy, clinging friends who tended to take more than they gave to the relationship. Though it might be a little painful, consider the following qualities of a good friend as they relate to your relationship with God. How do you rate? Mark each characteristic with a 5 (for "Always"), 4 ("Usually"), 3 ("Sometimes"), 2 ("Rarely"), or 1 ("Never").

_____   *Good listener:* Interested in how the other person is doing. Asks good questions. Hears the other person out; doesn't interrupt. Cares about that person's feelings. Comfortable with silence.

_____   *Low maintenance:* Isn't overly needy. Secure in self and friendship, not demanding. Doesn't need constant attention. Isn't threatened by time apart.

_____   *Not easily offended:* Patient when needs aren't immediately met. Believes the best, not the worst, of the other person. Doesn't jump to conclusions. Willing to talk things out.

_____   *Available:* Always there when needed. Willing to set aside own plans in order to help a friend. Returns calls quickly and doesn't ignore e-mails.

do his bidding and declare Himself king, Jesus responded with these amazing words: "Friend, do what you came for" (Matthew 26:50).

Friend? That name seems strange for a betrayer. Until you read it in the Greek. Then you realize Jesus was calling Judas exactly what he had proven himself to be.[10]

Hetairos. Selfish comrade. Opportunist. Groupie. Unfaithful, deceptive friend.

Lazarus or Judas? *Philos* or *hetairos*? Which one will we be?

In the end, it's up to us.

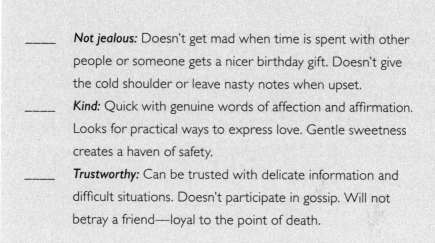

_____ **Not jealous:** Doesn't get mad when time is spent with other people or someone gets a nicer birthday gift. Doesn't give the cold shoulder or leave nasty notes when upset.

_____ **Kind:** Quick with genuine words of affection and affirmation. Looks for practical ways to express love. Gentle sweetness creates a haven of safety.

_____ **Trustworthy:** Can be trusted with delicate information and difficult situations. Doesn't participate in gossip. Will not betray a friend—loyal to the point of death.

Now count your points. A score of 29–35 suggests you are well on your way to being a true friend of God; 22–28 means you'd like to be a good friend but need some work; 14–21 means you probably didn't realize you were supposed to be God's friend; 7–13 means you just don't care.

(Note: If you scored low, you may find your human relationships are suffering as well. How we express our love for God directly affects our love for people—and vice versa.)

He who loves a pure heart and whose speech is gracious
will have the king for his friend.
PROVERBS 22:11

Loving Him or Loving Me?

I wonder. I just wonder.

What if the love-doubt, the chronic detachment, even the *hetairos* tendency that plagues so many of us as Christians could be solved by a simple mind change? an attitude shift? a softening and opening of a heart that's grown cold and hard?

I know of a woman who has never quite gotten around to accepting her husband's love. Because she grew up in a dysfunctional home, she's never felt worthy or very secure. Her husband has done everything he can to convince her of his love, yet nothing is ever enough.

"I just don't feel like he loves me," she whines, listing all the ways he's let her down, though the man works two or three jobs to be able to give her what she wants. She seems almost happy in her misery, because it's become her identity. As for her poor husband—well, he looks tired. Very tired. He won't leave her or their marriage. He loves her far too much. But I see him slowly stepping back rather than stepping up. Shrugging his shoulders at her displeasure with the weariness only hopelessness can bring.

They will stay married, but unless this woman opens her heart to her husband's love, I fear they will increasingly be strangers. Two lonely people sleeping in one bed with enough love to quench both drought-stricken souls if the one would only open her heart to its flow.

Her husband isn't the only one who suffers this person's demanding diatribes. Her heavenly Father receives His share as well. He's loved her long, and He's loved her well, but you wouldn't know it to talk to her. According to her, nothing He does is ever enough.

When one of His other children receives a blessing, she crosses her arms and turns up her nose. "Well, I guess God loves you better than He loves me," she says, pretending her sarcasm is only pretend. When someone else's prayers are answered, she comments cynically, "I guess I better have you pray. He certainly doesn't listen to me."

She isn't always this cynical. Sometimes, especially when (in her view) God is behaving, she's fairly joyous. But when things don't go her way, she's quick to bad-mouth God. She'd never admit it, of course. She believes she's simply stating the facts. But I've heard her bitter resentment, and others have too.

While I know God will never leave her, I can't help but wonder how He feels when He hears her slander His name. Weary, I'm certain. Discouraged perhaps. For God knows He can't force her to let Him love her. He can't demand she return His friendship. It's a choice only she can make.

Unlike her husband, however, God doesn't put up with spoiled, demanding divas. He disciplines them even as He loves them. But they may never come to appreciate His devotion, let alone feel it, if they continue to insist (either consciously or not): "He just doesn't love me the way I need to be loved."

Speaking Well of His Name

Isn't it strange how we humans tend to view God as our servant rather than our Master? Insisting that He do our bidding rather than standing ready to do His? It's no wonder we fail so often in the holy pursuit of being His friend.

"Here is a solemn thought for those who would be friends of God," Charles Haddon Spurgeon once wrote. "A man's friend must show himself friendly, and behave with tender care for his friend."[11]

Let me ask you a question. Do you speak well of God? Is His name safe on your tongue?

More and more I'm hearing Christians bad-mouth God. Rather than recalling what our heavenly Father has done for us in the past—His faithfulness and His goodness—we fixate on the unresolved problems of the present, thrashing about, accusing God of abandonment. Slandering His name rather than calling on it. Pushing away, rather than stepping toward, the love we so desperately need.

I understand how easy that is to do. Spiritual amnesia is a common condition among Christians. We've all suffered an unholy forgetfulness at times that eclipses any answered prayers or kindnesses received in the past. Like the Israelites of old, we tend to be slow to express gratitude when things are good yet quick to complain when things are bad. But if you and I are ever to be true friends of God, dear one, we need to start acting like one.

George Müller, one of the nineteenth century's greatest missionaries, opened hundreds of orphanages, taking in the indigent children of England. It wasn't an easy job. And yet he wrote at the end of his life, "In the greatest difficulties, in the heaviest trials, in the deepest poverty and necessities, [God] has never failed me; but because I was enabled by His grace to trust in Him, He has always appeared for my help. I delight in speaking well of His Name."[12]

Oh how I want that to be true of my life!

Last night, after being gone for a few days to write, I slipped back into town to spend the evening with John and Joshua.

Most kids, especially little kids, tend to make their parents pay for going away. Whether it's conscious or unconscious, they withdraw a bit, wanting you to know they're put out because you left them. Even if you left them with their dad. Even if he did fix them peanut-butter-and-jelly sandwiches every day, take them to the park, and spring for bowling and pizza one night and a video the next.

No, you surely abandoned them. So you must feel their pain.

I am so fortunate. Josh doesn't play games like that. Instead of sulking, he's the first one to meet me at the door.

"Mommy!" he cries as he rounds the corner and lunges into my arms. "I missed you!" Then pulling me into the living room, he tells me all about his day and the pizza and the bowling.

"I wuuuuv you," he says in his sweet, soft drawl, pressing close. As close as he can, until we're just one mushy heart sitting on a couch, sipping the love shared between us.

Josh doesn't greet me with a cold shoulder. He doesn't wait until I reach out for him. He leaps toward me.

That is the relationship, the friendship, Jesus longs to have with every one of us. And because of the Cross, a door has been opened into God's presence that allows us to run straight into His arms, joyfully claiming His gaga love for us. Singing with confidence the words of the wonderful old song:

Friendship with Jesus,
Fellowship divine;

Oh, what blessed sweet communion,

Jesus is a friend of mine.[13]

But true friendship must be reciprocated—a give-and-take of love on both sides. Anything less leads only to mere acquaintances.

Though I'm honored and privileged to have Jesus as my friend, my deepest desire is to be His friend as well. Proclaiming how much I love Him and then showing it in practical, visible ways. Laying down my wants and wishes that I might love my Savior with His best interests in mind.

A true *philos*. A genuine friend. Loyal and devoted.

From beginning to end.

Jesus loved Martha and her sister and Lazarus.
Yet when he heard that Lazarus was sick,
he stayed where he was two more days....
On his arrival, Jesus found that Lazarus had already
been in the tomb for four days....
When Martha heard that Jesus was coming,
she went out to meet him, but Mary stayed at home.
"Lord," Martha said to Jesus, "if you had been here,
my brother would not have died.
But I know that even now God will give you whatever you ask."....
"Where have you laid him?" [Jesus] asked.
"Come and see, Lord," they replied.
Jesus wept.

JOHN 11:5–6, 17, 20–22, 34–35

When Love Tarries

I remember how excited I was the morning of my twelfth Christmas. Of all the things I'd asked for, the one thing I really wanted was the one thing I actually needed (an advent of practicality I wouldn't experience again until my late thirties when my only Christmas wish was for a really good office chair).

That year all I wanted was a metronome—a mechanical device that my piano teacher promised would help my rhythm. Although I'd taken piano lessons for six years, I still struggled with one of the most important and fundamental principles of music. Keeping time.

The composition in front of me might call for adagio, which means "slowly." But I tended to play nearly everything allegro—"fast." Really, really fast. Once I got the notes down and my fingers learned their part, I'd attempt to follow the composer's directions at the top of the page. I'd try to interpret his or her vision for the piece. But eventually, no matter what the instructions, I allegroed everything. I just couldn't help it. And while I've improved a lot since my early days, I still tend to anticipate the beat.

In my defense I must say that long-ago Christmas gift wasn't a lot of help. Rather than performing the crisp *tick, tick, tick* its back-and-forth motion was designed to give, my new metronome had a little hitch in it. A hitch that was in direct opposition to the hitch in me. Rather than anticipating the count, the metronome seemed to pause a bit before sounding the next beat. Which really *tick, tick, tick*ed me off!

I had my mother take the metronome back to the store. I even complained to my teacher. But both sources told us the device was fine. Yes, the pause was a little annoying, they agreed, but the beat itself was right on time. I needed to adjust to the metronome, they told me, rather than demand it adjust to me.

That's a fundamental principle of life I'm still trying to learn—and a valuable one. Because, for some reason, God seems awfully fond of pauses. And nowhere is His propensity toward delay more evident than in the story of Lazarus.

THE INCONVENIENT PATIENCE OF LOVE

"Do you see anything yet?" I imagine Martha asking quietly as she joins her sister on the front porch. "Jesus should have been here by now, don't you think?"

But Mary doesn't answer. She can't. Turning away instead to hide her tears, she goes back into the house to check on their brother.

"Where are You, Lord?" Martha whispers as she gazes down the dirt road, looking for shapes on the horizon or, at the very least, a lone figure coming back with news of Jesus's pending arrival. But there is nothing—only one bird calling to another in the distance and the sun beating down on her head.

"Where are You?" Martha groans softly.

Suddenly a loud wail comes from the house behind her, and Martha knows her brother is gone. After a final desperate glance down the road, she rushes to find her sister collapsed at Lazarus's bedside, stroking and kissing his lifeless hand as tears course down her cheeks.

Why? The depth of sorrow in Mary's eyes magnifies Martha's own pain as her sister pleads for help to make sense of it all. "Why didn't Jesus come?" she asks. "Why did Lazarus have to die?"

But there are no answers—none that make sense. So the two sisters find comfort where they can. In each other's arms.

And in their pain we find echoes of our own confusion. As well as questions—so very many questions.

What are we to do when God doesn't behave the way we thought He should, the way we were taught He would? What are we to feel when our Savior seemingly pulls a no-show, leaving us to wrestle with the pain on our own?

These difficult times—these dark nights of the soul[1]—rattle our convictions and shake the foundations of our faith. Author Brian Jones writes about such a crisis in his book *Second Guessing God:*

The year before I graduated from seminary, I lost my faith in God. That's not a smart thing to do, I'll admit. There's not a big job market out there for pastors who are atheists. But I couldn't help it. Life was becoming too painful. Truth had become too open to interpretation.... My doubts seemed to climb on top of one another, clamoring for attention. Before I knew what had happened, the new car smell of my faith had worn off, and I found myself fighting to hang on.[2]

After reading every book he could find on the existence of God and enduring months of sleepless nights, Jones reached the point of panic attacks and deep depression, even thoughts of suicide. One night, frantic, he called a former professor who had been a mentor to him.

"In the last six months doubt has begun to paralyze me," he told the older man. "It's like when the water goes back out to the ocean. [Doubt] is washing away the sand underneath me, and my feet keep sinking lower and lower and lower. If this keeps up, there won't be anything left to stand on."[3]

Rather than reacting with a sermon on the necessity of faith, the wise professor acknowledged Brian's struggle, even sharing his own battle against unbelief. But then he added these final words: "Brian, listen to me when I say this. When the last grain of sand is finally gone, you're going to discover that you're standing on a rock."[4]

"That one sentence saved me," Jones writes. It helped him hold on long enough to eventually rediscover hope.[5]

No, his doubts weren't obliterated overnight, but the professor's words provided Jones enough light to start heading back home. Away from the wilderness of wondering and wandering, back to the only place that's truly safe.

The heart of God.

DOES HE LOVE ME?

In John 11:5–6 we see this strange paradox: "Jesus *loved* Martha and her sister and Lazarus. *Yet* when he heard that Lazarus was sick, he *stayed* where he was two more days" (emphasis added).

Jesus loved…yet He stayed where he was.

He loved…but He didn't show up when He was expected.

How can that be? our hearts cry. It just doesn't make sense.

And that is the core of the issue, isn't it? Because most of the love-doubt we feel can be traced back to troubling contradictions not unlike the one in the story of Lazarus. Inconsistencies like the ones Brian Jones experienced. Doubts that eat away at the bedrock of our faith, leaving us floundering, gasping for air as we try to keep our spiritual heads above water.

I'm sure the sorrow Mary and Martha felt must have threatened to swamp all they knew and believed about Jesus. It certainly left them shaken.

John 11:20 tells us, "When Martha heard that Jesus was coming, she went out to meet him, but Mary stayed at home."

Two different responses from two very different sisters—and unexpected ones, at that. Strangely, it was the sister who had once questioned Jesus's love ("Lord, don't you care?" Luke 10:40) who now went running toward Him. While the sister who had sat at the Master's feet in sweet communion remained in the house, paralyzed by grief.

Why do you suppose they reacted so differently?

I have no way of knowing for sure, but I believe it was because Martha had already gone through a testing of faith, while Mary was just entering that crucible process (as eventually all of us do).

As strange as it might sound, it may have been the Lord's denial of what Martha had wanted earlier in their relationship that allowed her to find what her heart needed most on that grief-filled day.

Rather than responding with practical help when she'd demanded more assistance in the kitchen, Jesus had simply replied, "Martha, Martha, you are worried and upset about many things, but only one thing is needed" (Luke 10:41–42). With those words He'd exposed Martha's biggest problem—and her deepest need.

She hadn't needed more help in the kitchen. She'd needed the "one thing"— Jesus Himself. Though His rebuke must have hurt, I believe Martha took His words to heart. As she humbled herself and embraced the Lord's correction, her heart was enabled to embrace His love. No wonder she was the sister who ran down the road to meet Jesus after her brother died.

Somewhere in that earlier time of testing, I believe Martha discovered three marvelous, indomitable truths we all need to know. Three rock-solid facts on which we too can rest our hearts:

1. God is *love*—therefore I am loved.
2. God is *good*—therefore I am safe.
3. God is *faithful*—therefore it's going to be okay. For God is incapable of doing anything less than marvelous things.[6]

Martha chose to trust God's love and His faithful goodness. Because of that, when tough times came, she was able to trust His sovereignty as well—His right to do as He deems best, when and how He wants to do it.

That's why she could run to Jesus, fall at His feet, and pour out her heart with both pain and sweet abandon. "Lord," she cried, "if you had been here, my brother would not have died. But I know that even now God will give you whatever you ask" (John 11:21–22).

Here is the quill of my will, Lord, Martha was saying. You *write the end of the story. For You do all things well.*

Surrendering the quill of my will has always been a difficult process for me. You see, I have such good ideas about how my story, not to mention the stories of the people I love, should be written. Always Daddy's little helper, I'm quick to provide God with lists of alternate ideas in case my Plan A doesn't match up with His. "You don't care for that one, Lord? Well, how about Plans B, C, D, and E? Why, I even have a Plan Z if you'd like more details."

Unfortunately, none of my planning and plotting has ever drawn me closer to God. In fact, it usually does the opposite.

While I'm busy scheming, my Father is apt to move on, leaving me to work the angles on my own. *That wasn't my plan, Joanna,* He gently whispers when I finally call out to Him. *If you want to walk with Me, you have to surrender your itinerary and trust Mine.*

Surrender was the key to Martha's amazing transformation, and it is the key to ours as well. For whenever we choose to give up our agendas and submit to God's plan, we release Him to have His way in our lives. More important, when we choose to pursue the "one thing" of knowing Christ rather than continually choosing to do "our own thing," we discover the great depths of His love just as Martha did.

Unfortunately, these concepts are easy to talk about and much harder to live out. Especially when God's timing runs contrary to our own.

WHO'S FOLLOWING WHOM?

My son Joshua loves music. Every once in a while, I'll catch him bobbing his head or bouncing around in his chair. "Whatcha doing, honey?" I'll ask.

"Oh, I'm just dancing to the music in my head," he'll reply with a sheepish grin.

What an adorable pastime—for a little boy. But it's not such a good practice for a full-grown adult like me. Because, as I've mentioned, the music in my head often proves faulty, especially when it comes to following a beat.

It's been a while since I've played piano with a worship band. It's proven too traumatic for everyone involved, especially the poor drummers. My anticipation of the downbeat tends to turn the most mellow musicians into *tick, tick, tick*ing time bombs of pure frustration. So most of the time, out of a desire not to cause people to sin, I elect to sit out.

But our new church's sound system has nifty headphones that allow the drummer to block out the piano, if need be, and the pianist to turn up the drummer, if she prefers. So these days, with their help I occasionally try playing with the band.

My tendency to anticipate the downbeat is as strong as ever, but I'm learning to play with the tempo, rather than against it, by

- turning up the beat in my headphones,
- relinquishing control to the drummer,
- relaxing into the flow of the music set by him.

Because here's the deal. Joe, our drummer, has rhythm. I do not—unless I choose to follow his lead.

I'm trying to learn that in my Christian walk as well. If I'll move to the beat of the Spirit and relinquish control of my life to Him, I'll be able to dance to the music God has playing in *His* head rather than movin' and agroovin' to the catchy little tunes I've got going in my own. For when I allow the Lord to provide the accompaniment to my life, I discover a richly layered soundtrack more beautiful than anything I could compose myself.

But following God's beat, dancing to His rhythm, trusting in His sovereignty—all that can be hard for a rhythmically challenged, control-loving person like me. Because when it comes right down to it, I'm a headstrong little girl who wants her own way in pretty much every area of life.

Fortunately, I have a Father who loves me in spite of that. But while He loves me as I am, He also loves me too much to leave me that way. So He insists I follow His lead in order to "grow up" in my salvation (1 Peter 2:2). Becoming more like Jesus and less like me.

The Art of Waiting

Have you ever felt the need to rush ahead of God? All through Scripture we are encouraged to develop the all-important—and really difficult—art of waiting. Warren Wiersbe shares three statements in Scripture that have helped him hone prayerful patience in his own life—principles he applies whenever he feels nervous about a situation and is tempted to hurry God:

1. "*Stand still,* and see the salvation of the LORD" (Exodus 14:13, NKJV).
2. "*Sit still*...until you know how the matter will turn out" (Ruth 3:18, NKJV).
3. "*Be still,* and know that I am God" (Psalm 46:10).

"When you wait on the Lord in prayer," Wiersbe writes, "you are not wasting your time; you are investing it. God is preparing both you and your circumstances so that His purposes will be accomplished. However, when the right time arrives for us to act by faith, we dare not delay."[7]

But they that wait upon the LORD shall renew their strength;
they shall mount up with wings as eagles;
they shall run, and not be weary;
and they shall walk, and not faint.

ISAIAH 40:31, KJV

And therein lies another problem. Because growing up, my friend, can be hard to do.

BEING A BIG GIRL

From the moment we're born, we tend to associate love with what others do (or do not do) for us and the speed with which they do it. We learn to feel loved when we get our needs met—quickly.

And that's appropriate...for babies.

Unfortunately, a lot of us never outgrow that view of love. When we cry (or whine creatively, as I like to call it), we expect an immediate response.

The Blessing of Trouble

Of all the hard sayings of the Bible, perhaps none is as difficult to understand as Jesus's response to Lazarus's death in John 11:15. "For your sake I am glad I was not there," He tells the disciples. But then He adds the reason: "so that you may believe." Jesus knows that some of life's greatest gifts come wrapped in disappointments, and faith is often learned best in the crucible of pain. Listen to Charles Haddon Spurgeon's thoughts on this verse:

> If you want to ruin your son, never let him know a hardship. When he is a child carry him in your arms, when he becomes a youth still dandle him, and when he becomes a man still dry-nurse him, and you will succeed in producing an arrant fool. If you want to prevent his being made useful in the world, guard him from every kind of toil. Do not suffer him to struggle. Wipe the sweat from his dainty brow and say, "Dear child, thou shalt never have another task so arduous." Pity him when he ought to be punished; supply all his wishes, avert all disappointments, prevent all troubles, and you will surely tutor him to be a reprobate and to break your heart. But put him where he must work, expose him to difficulties,

"I'm dying of thirst," I tell my destination-focused husband as we travel down the interstate on vacation.

"You're not dying," he says calmly (though after so many years of marriage, you'd think he'd know this isn't the response I'm looking for).

What I want is for John to immediately look for the next exit and the closest minimart. *If he* really *loved me,* I think (and occasionally comment out loud), *he'd phone ahead to make sure they have the diet drink I prefer as well as a four-star rest room to accommodate the last Big Gulp I gulped down.*

Okay, I'm not that bad...usually. But, sadly, I sometimes carry the same childish, demanding spirit into my relationship with God. Not as often as I used to, however, because like my husband, my heavenly Father has proven difficult to manipulate.

purposely throw him into peril, and in this way you shall make him a man, and when he comes to do man's work and to bear man's trial, he shall be fit for either. My Master does not daintily cradle His children when they ought to run alone; and when they begin to run He is not always putting out His finger for them to lean upon, but He lets them tumble down to the cutting of their knees, because then they will walk more carefully by-and-by, and learn to stand upright by the strength which faith confers upon them.

You see, dear friends, that Jesus Christ was glad—glad that His disciples were blessed by trouble. Will you think of this, you who are so troubled this morning, Jesus Christ does sympathize with you, but still He does it wisely, and He says, "I am glad for your sakes that I was not there."[8]

No discipline seems pleasant at the time, but painful.
Later on, however, it produces a harvest of righteousness and peace
for those who have been trained by it.
HEBREWS 12:11

You see, God knows that if He indulged my insatiable desire to have instantaneous help at each and every juncture, I would never grow up. Not really. Instead, I'd be crippled emotionally and unable to stand, let alone walk, on my own.

Growing to maturity means learning to accept delayed gratification. Children and adults alike must learn to

- adapt to less-than-perfect situations,
- wait for the fulfillment of their needs,
- accept not only delays but also denials of what they want.

For anything less results in demanding divas and toddler terrorists.

"When I was a child," Paul writes in 1 Corinthians 13:11, "I talked like a child, I thought like a child, I reasoned like a child. When I became a man, I put childish ways behind me." Part of putting childish ways behind us, spiritually speaking, involves setting aside our misconception that if God loves us, He must act according to our specifications, our scripts, and especially our time lines.

Why is this important? Consider Paul's words in verse 12: "Now we see but a poor reflection as in a mirror; then we shall see face to face. Now I know in part; then I shall know fully, even as I am fully known."

Whether we realize it or not, we see only a small part of a very big picture. God, on the other hand, sees it all. That's why He refuses to operate solely on our recommendations. While we are encouraged to bring our needs and even our creative whining to Him—to "come boldly to the throne of grace" with full assurance that He hears and answers our prayers (Hebrews 4:16, NKJV)—we must leave the responses to our requests up to Him.

For if we are ever to get past our love-doubt, we must accept the reality that God's answers are not always the answers we are looking for. Instead of saying yes to all our requests, like a wise parent, God often chooses to say no.

And sometimes, as in the case of Lazarus, His answer is...wait awhile.

A Long Time to Wait

According to the Bible, when Jesus arrived in Bethany, Lazarus had been dead for four days. Why did Jesus choose to wait so long before resurrecting His friend?

Some scholars say it was to counteract the Jewish belief that the soul hovers over the body for three days before departing.[9] That explains why grieving families often delayed entombment—to avoid the unlikely but tragic possibility of burying someone alive. Within three days the soul might still reenter the body. But four days? Well, four days meant all hope was gone. It was time to let go and move on.

So Jesus's delay makes sense, I suppose. But I confess to wondering if it was really necessary for Jesus to put His friends through all that painful waiting. Couldn't He have done it a different way?

You could ask the same question about a lot of stories in the Bible.

Was it really necessary to leave Joseph rotting in an Egyptian prison cell for such an extended period? Was it vitally important that the Israelites wander in the desert for forty years and Noah drift on a flood for months in a boat that took perhaps a century to build? Were twenty-five years really necessary to get Abraham from the promise to Pampers? Surely there had to be simpler, not to mention faster, methods by which to fulfill God's purposes.

Now, it could be argued that many of the extended delays outlined above were caused by the people themselves. If Joseph hadn't bragged to his brothers and if the Israelites had believed God rather than their doubting eyes and if Abraham hadn't pulled an Ishmael, who knows what the trajectories of their journeys might have looked like? After all, did the ark really require one hundred years of construction, or was Noah just a procrastinator like me with a tendency to view God's mandate as more of a hobby than an actual career?

We just don't know. But the good news I find in all these stories is the astounding truth that no matter what happens, God's plans always eventually succeed. Despite our stumblings and fumblings and even our outright rebellion, our mighty God will accomplish His work one way or another.

Though it seems to me He could find better resources, God consistently chooses to do it through you and me. Whether we follow willingly (though imperfectly) or have to be dragged kicking and screaming to our own personal Nineveh by a proverbial whale, "it is the Lord's purpose that prevails" (Proverbs 19:21).

But please know that while God is committed to His plans, He is not insensitive to our pain. We are not pawns in some celestial chess match. We are His children, "chosen...and dearly loved" (Colossians 3:12).

Loved, in fact, to the point of tears.

Jesus wept, remember, as He stood before Lazarus's tomb (John 11:35).

While theologians disagree about what may have caused Jesus's tears—some attributing it to anger over what sin had done to the world and others to the lack of faith in the people around Him—I believe it was love that made Jesus weep. Though He knew His friend would soon walk out completely well and fully alive, the Lord still mourned along with the family He counted so dear.

He felt their pain, but His own heart broke as well.

Enduring Love

When the writer of John 11:6 tells us that Jesus stayed where He was two days longer, he uses the Greek word *meno*. "This term not only means that he stayed—or tarried—two days more," Jerry Goebel writes, "it also means he *endured* two more days. This adds great meaning to the verse. It tells us how difficult it was for Jesus to hold Himself back from rushing to Lazarus' side."[10]

Ah, the great restraint of God. We rarely think about how hard it must be for a Father who loves us so much to hold back from running constantly to our rescue. Yet in His merciful wisdom He does, because He knows there is a greater good and a higher plan at work.

Jesus Himself consistently resisted pleas to speed up His work, choosing instead to live by heaven's metronome. He refused to be pushed into a miracle by His mother (John 2:4), and He wouldn't be goaded by His brothers into going to Jerusalem before His time (John 7:6–10). Though our Lord eventually did both, He did them according to the timetable given by His Father, not at the prompting of demanding voices around Him.

So when Jesus told the disciples, "Lazarus is dead, and for your sake I am glad I was not there, so that you may believe" (John 11:14–15), He was declaring His purpose as well as His love. It wasn't that He didn't care. He was simply pointing out that there was a whole lot more at stake than His friends knew. The stage was being set for Jesus to be crucified and God to be glorified. And all of it—the tragedy and the triumph, the sorrow and the joy—was part of what would become the foundation of your faith and mine.[11]

For *"at just the right time,"* Paul writes in Romans 5:6, "when we were still powerless, Christ died for the ungodly" (emphasis added). The events leading up to the Cross didn't happen too soon. Nor did they take place too late.

And neither do the events of our lives, no matter how it may feel. If we'll rest in God's goodness and trust His perfect, sovereign timing, we'll be able to say along with David, "My times are in your hands" (Psalm 31:15). Even when the hourglass seems to be running out and waiting proves the most difficult work we do.

For you can't rush a resurrection, nor can you hurry God along. He has His own internal speedometer, and as much as we'd like it, there is no pedal to push when we wish He'd pick up the pace.

However, we can count on this: God is at work. Though it seems we're walking toward a funeral, something marvelous is waiting on the other side.

A brand-new life, four days in the making.

Christ revealed in you and me so that the whole world might see.

Moving Beyond Why

One of the most powerful testimonies I've ever heard came from a man born with cerebral palsy. David Ring is an evangelist and a powerful communicator even though, at first, his words are difficult to understand. When you listen closely, however, you are drawn into a message that is nothing less than transformative.

"Why, Mama?" David used to ask his mother when school kids teased him. "Why did I have to be born this way?" Although exceptionally bright, he was caught in a body that wouldn't do his bidding and constantly tripped up by a stuttering tongue.

God gave that sweet mother incredible wisdom as she taught her son that perhaps *why* wasn't the best question after all.

"Asking why is like going to a well with a bucket and coming up empty every time," Ring's mother told him. Instead, she said, the question should be, "What can I become?"[12]

What a powerful, life-changing concept for all of us, especially when we're trapped and tripped up by the whys of life. Because when it comes right down to it, life is full of questions that don't have adequate answers.

Why are some children born healthy and others are not?

Why do some mothers have to scrounge for food in sub-Saharan Africa, while mothers like me struggle to choose from endless aisles of endless food in grocery stores just around the corner?

Why do good and godly people die slow and painful deaths while others, depraved and careless, enjoy long lives padded with bulging bank accounts and multiple vacation homes?

Why does it sometimes seem that God has forgotten us?

Such questions haunted the writers of the Old Testament. "Why have you forsaken me?" cried the psalmist (Psalm 22:1). "Why does the way of the wicked prosper?" the prophet Jeremiah asked (Jeremiah 12:1). And again, "Why did I ever come out of the womb to see trouble and sorrow and to end my days in shame?" (Jeremiah 20:18).

Those questions haunted my friend Tom as well.[13] Tom was a sweet kid who started coming to our church as an eleven-year-old. His mom, who struggled with addictions, often drank away the rent money, and Tom lived in fear that they would be kicked out on the street. During his teen years he stayed with us from time to time.

Though Tom loved Jesus, he struggled with his own temptations, especially with the whys of his difficult life. But I'll never forget the morning he came bounding upstairs, his sixteen-year-old face smiling as only Tom can smile. "I figured it out, Mama Jo!" he said. "Now I know why my life is the way it is."

With a huge grin he handed me his Bible and pointed to where he'd been reading. It was the story from John 9 where Jesus healed a man who had been born blind. The disciples (and almost everyone else) assumed that sin—either that of the blind man or his parents—was to blame for the man's disability. But Jesus said otherwise, and that's what had Tom so excited.

"Look, Mama," he said, pointing at the verse, then pointing at himself with a smile as we read it together.

"This happened so that the work of God might be displayed in his life" (John 9:3).

Oh that we all might have vision to see beyond the misery of what is to the miracle of what we can become. But that kind of foresight comes only through surrender. Through laying down our wants and wishes so we might live for God's alone.

In the Meantime

Four days is a long time to wait for a resurrection, especially when you feel that all hope is gone. Figuratively, you may be living in those dark 96 hours before dawn, wondering if the 5,760 minutes will ever end. Each of the 345,600 seconds that make up your waiting seems to hold its breath interminably, like my malfunctioning metronome, leaving you suspended between faith and doubt. Wondering if the dissonant chord hanging over your life will ever be resolved.

Four days is a long time to wait. I know. I've endured their incessant length myself.

But believe me, none of it is wasted time.

Although we may be "hard pressed on every side," Paul reminds us in 2 Corinthians 4:8–9, we are not crushed. Though we may feel "perplexed," we are not in despair. Though we are "persecuted," we are not abandoned. Though "struck down," we are not destroyed.

Instead, the apostle—beaten and stoned, shipwrecked three times—reminds us that we "carry around in our body the death of Jesus, so that the life of Jesus may also be revealed in our body" (verse 10).

Don't you love the creative irony of God! Paul is telling us that the very circumstances and events we believe will destroy us, the ones that generate so many of our whys, can actually serve as catalysts for the full manifestation of Christ in our lives— Jesus more accurately revealed in you and me. After all, as 1 Peter 1:7 reminds us, these trials "have come so that your faith—of greater worth than gold, which perishes even though refined by fire—may be proved genuine and may result in praise, glory and honor when *Jesus Christ is revealed*" (emphasis added).

In other words, don't get so caught up in what's happening that you miss what is really going on.[14] For if we'll listen for the beat of a different Drummer and relinquish control of our lives to His loving, sovereign lead, nothing will be wasted.

Not the waiting, not our questions, not even our pain.

For when you can't trace God's hand, you can trust His heart.

On his arrival, Jesus found that Lazarus had already
been in the tomb for four days.
Bethany was less than two miles from Jerusalem,
and many Jews had come to Martha and Mary to comfort
them in the loss of their brother.
When Martha heard that Jesus was coming, she went
out to meet him, but Mary stayed at home.
"Lord," Martha said to Jesus, "if you had been here,
my brother would not have died.
But I know that even now God will give you whatever you ask."....
When Jesus saw [Mary] weeping, and the Jews who had come
along with her also weeping,
he was deeply moved in spirit and troubled.
"Where have you laid him?" [Jesus] asked.
"Come and see, Lord," they replied.
Jesus wept.

<small>JOHN 11:17–22, 33–35</small>

Tomb Dwelling

I 'll never forget my first visit to New Orleans more than a decade ago. It was before the tragedy of Hurricane Katrina, so the city I encountered was full of life. I enjoyed powdered-sugar beignets at the Café Du Monde, browsed quaint antique shops, and listened to street musicians playing every flavor of jazz imaginable. But of all the sights I saw—the antebellum mansions, the horse-drawn carriages, the paddleboats with their giant wheels patiently treading the Mississippi—it is the cemeteries that I remember most.

Because the city is built below sea level, normal burials are impossible in most of New Orleans. "The coffins eventually float to the surface," the tour guide told us as we passed one enormous graveyard. "That's the reason for the above-ground mausoleums, both individual ones and large ones that hold entire families."

Though the tour bus drove by the cemetery quickly, the sight was graphic and a little disturbing. I couldn't get past the loneliness and haunting sadness that seemed to shroud the graveyard like the Spanish moss dripping from the trees. And that was in broad daylight.

I can't begin to imagine what it would be like to visit a place like that at night... let alone live there.

LIVING AMONG TOMBS

One of the things I love most about Jesus is that He seeks us out wherever we may be. He never tires of going out of His way to find us, crossing stormy seas as well as eternity just to make us His own.

Luke 8:22 tells us that "one day Jesus said to his disciples, 'Let's go over to the other side of the lake.' " According to the parallel time line given in Matthew, He had just finished a busy couple of weeks. After preaching the Sermon on the Mount to thousands (Matthew 5–7), Jesus healed a leper, then traveled to Capernaum to heal a suffering paralytic and Peter's fevered mother-in-law (8:1–15). That same evening, according to Matthew, "many who were demon-possessed were brought to him, and he drove out the spirits with a word and healed all the sick" (8:16).

It was after this exhausting schedule that Jesus gave the order to cross to the other side of the lake. But what might appear at first glance to be a weary man's attempt to get away from a demanding crowd was actually nothing of the kind. Jesus wasn't suggesting an escape route. He was simply moving toward the next destination God had logged into the navigational guide of His ministry from the beginning of time.

Though a crowd of needy people remained on one side of the lake, Jesus left them all in order to meet the needs of an individual on the other side. One lonely, tormented soul living on the outskirts of civilization. In a graveyard.

Listen to how Mark 5:2–5 describes the scene:

When Jesus got out of the boat, a man with an evil spirit came from the tombs to meet Him. This man lived in the tombs, and no one could bind him any more, not even with a chain. For he had often been chained hand and foot, but he tore the chains apart and broke the irons on his feet. No one was strong enough to subdue him. Night and day among the tombs and in the hills he would cry out and cut himself with stones.

What a sad, eerie picture of a tormented life. And yet when the man saw Jesus, he ran and fell at His feet. "What do you want with me, Jesus, Son of the Most High God?" he shouted at the top of his voice. "Swear to God that you won't torture me!" (verse 7).

Isn't it amazing how the very thing we need is often the last thing we want? Here was a man who lived surrounded by death. Yet when he encountered the Lord of Life, the one and only One who could deliver him, he didn't call out for help. Instead, self-preservation was his first response. "What do you want with me? Don't torture me!"

Now, I realize it was the demons in the man who spoke these words. Yet I think it's important to note that Satan often uses the same arguments to keep us from surrendering to the work of God in our lives. *It will be too painful,* he hisses. *Why doesn't He just leave you alone? There's no hope for you anyway.*

It's much easier to stay in your bondage, he suggests. *Sure, you roam the graveyard of your past day and night, trying to find answers. Sure, your mind is tormented as you mutilate yourself in an attempt to obliterate the pain. You can't sleep, and at times you cry uncontrollably. But that's a whole lot less painful than what God has in store for you,* the Deceiver insinuates. *Who knows what God might make you do if you allowed Him to set you free?*

Does any of this sound familiar to you? I know it does to me. For many of us have spent more time among the tombs than we'd care to admit.

Caught Between Death and Life

According to scholars it wasn't unusual for tombs around Israel to be inhabited by the poor or the insane. Graveyards were sometimes the only places where outcasts could find shelter.[1]

Dug into hillsides or straight into the ground, many tombs in Jesus's day were made up of two chambers. The first room, sometimes called a vestibule, held a simple stone seat, while the inner chamber featured a carved-out niche (or niches) where the body was laid.[2] After waiting a year for decay to do its work, the bones would be placed in an ossuary, a stone box, thus making the tomb available when another member of the family passed away.[3]

I'm assuming the outcasts must have made their home in the vestibule. It served as a kind of middle ground—protected from the outside elements yet not quite in the place of death.

Unfortunately, this "midchamber" describes the place where many of us live, metaphorically speaking. Suspended halfway between death and life, we've accepted the Lord as our Savior, but we have yet to step out into the fullness of life Christ

Hurts, Hang-ups, and Habits

The Celebrate Recovery program coined the phrase "hurts, hang-ups, and habits" to describe the things that keep us from true freedom. Consider these three categories (the definitions are mine). Ask the Holy Spirit to reveal anything that may be acting as a stronghold in your life.[4]

Hurts
(painful things that have happened to us)

These are events we keep referring back to, situations that have defined us. Whatever has wounded us has the capacity to keep us bound. (Examples: trauma, abuse, abandonment, bereavement, failure)

Hang-ups
(mental blocks and emotional barriers that cause unhealthy attitudes and patterns of behavior)

These affect the ways we respond to experiences and act toward people. They are often motivated by anger or fear. (Examples: passive-aggressiveness, chronic people pleasing, rage, bigotry)

Habits
(addictions and compulsive behaviors we've turned to so often that they've become a part of us)

Whether the habit is primarily *physical* or *emotional,* it has become ingrained through repetition and exerts a control we feel helpless to break. (Examples: alcoholism, drug addiction, eating disorders, overspending, pornography)

"But I will restore you to health and heal your wounds,"
declares the LORD.
JEREMIAH 30:17

came to give. Instead, we're holed up in the dark, held captive by our hurts, our hang-ups, and our habits.[5] The painful memories we just can't shake. The attitudes that keep us bound. The coping mechanisms we continually return to, though they lead us everywhere but to the heart of God.

"Strongholds," the Bible calls them (2 Corinthians 10:4). And it's a good name, for they truly have a strong hold on us.

Which may explain the spiritual inertia many Christians apparently feel. According to the Willow Creek Association's REVEAL survey of churches, over 20 percent of respondents were honest enough to admit they feel "stalled" in their walk with God. While they aren't necessarily stepping back from their faith, they realize they aren't moving forward. And that concerns them. As it should.[6]

Because if we are ever to experience abundant life in Jesus, we must give God access to anything that holds us back, including the skeletons in our closets and the dark corners of our minds. For He wants to help us "demolish strongholds...and every pretension that sets itself up against the knowledge of God" (2 Corinthians 10:4–5).

Tombs-R-Us

It may seem a little strange to think that believers could still be tomb dwellers. But I think we've all felt the intense struggle of shedding our "old self" so that we might experience the "new self" Paul writes about in Ephesians 4:22–24. Strongholds are simply those places in us where sin and the "old self" have established such an immense power base that we feel helpless to escape their control. We love Jesus, but we remain stuck in our midchambers, unable to live free.

So where do you feel stuck in your Christian walk?

What hurt keeps you emotionally bound, frozen at a point of past failure or pain?

What hang-up keeps tripping you up, ensnaring you time and time again?

What habit or behavior controls you, making you feel perpetually defeated and continually undone? (See Appendix E: "Identifying Strongholds.")

I find it interesting that in the Greek, the root of the word for "tombs" means "to recall or remember."[7] For isn't it true that the majority of our strongholds have their origins in our pasts? Whether because of a long-ago experience or a regret from yesterday afternoon, too many of us travel through life with hurt and anger or guilt and condemnation shadowing our every move.

In a sense we're like the tormented man of Mark 5. We live in graveyards filled with memories. Wandering through life in perpetual mourning over the things we have done and the things that have been done to us. We may do our best to outrun the mistakes and regrets, the hurts and disappointments, but apart from God, we find it difficult to escape the cycle of shame and self-hatred that keeps our "sin...ever before" us (Psalm 51:3, KJV). Unfortunately, the coping mechanisms we embrace in order to manage our pain only reinforce the strongholds in our souls.

That's why Paul prayed that we might be sanctified and made holy "through and through"—spirit, soul, and body (1 Thessalonians 5:23). For although Christ has been enthroned in our spirits, there are kingdoms in our souls that have yet to receive the good news. Places in our minds, wills, and emotions that must be brought under His control.

Because any arena in our lives where Satan feels relatively comfortable is a stronghold from which we need to be set free. A tomb God wants to open.

Whether you struggle to escape a grave of your own making or one imposed on you by outside forces, I can tell you that each and every stronghold in your life was originally outsourced by hell itself. It isn't so much that Satan dislikes you personally. He simply despises God. He will go to any lengths to hurt, wound, and grieve the Father's heart. For you, dearly beloved, happen to be the apple of God's eye (Zechariah 2:8). It's your reflection Satan sees every time he looks at the heart of God. No wonder that from the moment you were born, he has studied you to determine—and target—your weak spots.

Are you shy by nature? Well, then, he'll make sure you are humiliated regularly to reinforce your fear of people. Are you prone to worry and anxiety? He'll make sure that it seems everything and everyone is against you. Do you struggle with pride and anger? He'll make sure that people know how to push your buttons—and that they do it with great frequency!

Why would the enemy of your soul go to all that trouble, you ask? As I wrote in a previous book, I'm convinced that Satan isn't nearly as concerned about losing you from *his* kingdom as he is committed to keeping you from being effective in *God's* kingdom. He has as many different methods as there are individuals, but his one goal is to contain and restrain you. To entomb you so he can consume you. To incarcerate you with so many lies, insecurities, and guilt feelings that the gift God intended your life to be remains undiscovered. Tightly wrapped and left forgotten in a corner cell.

How does he do it? Doubt by doubt, insult by insult, Satan puts backward binoculars to our eyes and distorts our worth and potential until we forget to factor in God. Until, like the Israelites, we say, "We seemed like grasshoppers in our own eyes, and we looked the same to [the enemy]" (Numbers 13:33).

Gleefully, the Accuser sews tight seams across our souls in an attempt to redefine us, hemming us in with tiny little stitches that diminish our lives and dismantle our faith.

This is who you are, he hisses as he bites off the thread. *This is all you'll ever be,* he gloats, turning us inside out to hide leftover fabric as he creates our burial shrouds. Doing his best to convince us how very small he says we are.

FIGHTING FOR LIFE

I received a letter not long ago from a concerned reader. While she enjoyed my books, she felt I gave too much credit to the devil. Didn't I know that Jesus had conquered Satan when He rose from the dead?

I wrote back and assured her that, yes, I did. In fact, Jesus's triumph over Satan is a cornerstone of my faith. I believe Christ not only conquered death through His resurrection; He also demolished the works of Satan and thoroughly humiliated him in the process. The Message paraphrase describes the victorious event so beautifully: "[Christ] stripped all the spiritual tyrants in the universe of their sham authority at the Cross and marched them naked through the streets" (Colossians 2:15).

In other words, Satan has absolutely no power over you and me.

But please, dear friend, don't be surprised when he tries to convince you otherwise.

Even though the devil's ultimate destiny and eventual destruction have been predetermined, he's still doing his best to stir up trouble. First Peter 5:8 tells us, "Your enemy the devil prowls around like a roaring lion looking for someone to devour." That lion has been detoothed and declawed by Christ's work on the cross, but he still howls and prowls this earth, looking for ways to intimidate God's children.

Rick Renner describes it like this in his excellent devotional *Sparkling Gems from the Greek.*

> Because of Jesus' death on the Cross and His resurrection from the dead, the forces of hell are *already* defeated. However, even though they have been legally stripped of their authority and power, they continue to roam around this earth, carrying out evil deeds like criminals, bandits, hooligans, and thugs. And just like criminals who refuse to submit to the law, these evil spirits will continue to operate in this world until some believer uses his God-given authority to enforce their defeat![8]

I want to learn how to use that authority. I don't want to live enslaved to a tyrant who no longer has a right to demean and terrorize me, tormenting me with guilt and self-doubt. I'm tired of giving the devil more airtime in my mind than I give the Holy Spirit.

My friend Kathy stopped listening to Satan's lies several years ago, and the change in her life has been amazing to see. Somewhat shy by nature, as a child she had let ridicule from schoolmates convince her she was better off quiet. Really quiet. So much so that Kathy became a professional wallflower. Always on the outside looking in, she hardly spoke and rarely participated at school. Even after she dedicated her life to Christ and became involved in ministry, it was always behind the scenes. She was the worker bee. Someone else could be the queen.

But as Kathy began getting into the Word, the Holy Spirit began illuminating her life, helping her see it differently. She came to realize she'd been living halfway since early childhood, stuck for decades in a midchamber of fear and rejection. As Kathy acknowledged her need for healing, God began to stir a courage within her that created a small strand of hope. Perhaps, just perhaps, there could be life beyond the tomb she'd settled for.

It's been my personal joy to watch my friend emerge from her tomb like a beautiful butterfly from a cocoon. No longer in the shadows, Kathy teaches women's Bible studies and has served as women's ministry director for our former church, coordinating and emceeing several large events.

All because she stopped cooperating with Satan's attempts to hem her in, shut her down, and close her off from the life God intended her to live.

Tomb Living—What's in It for You?

As I write these words, I have a wooden box sitting in front of me. About seven inches high and thirteen inches square, it is stained a rich walnut color, and is actually quite beautiful. Just looking at it reminds me of an epiphany I had while using it at a conference for pastors' wives several years ago.

"Each one of us contains so much potential," I told the women, holding up the box, "so many gifts God wants to share with the world. When we give Him access to every part of our hearts, the Holy Spirit causes our lives to open to all the possibilities God has placed within us." To show that truth, I'd designed the sides of the box to drop down and lie flat. I showed it to the women completely open and available, ready to showcase any treasure placed within.

"But Satan is aware of our potential as well," I added. "He goes out of his way to keep us from opening up. In fact, he'll do whatever it takes to derail God's plans and obscure His purposes for us."

With those words I began to close the box lying open before me.

"Satan wants to hem you in…" I pulled two sides upright. The sound of wood against wood rang sharply across the room.

"He wants to shut you down…" I slapped two more sides into place.

Then taking the matching lid, I slammed it down on top. "And he wants to close you off."

At the force of the lid coming down, a small shudder echoed through the room—and through our hearts as well. Every one of us had felt the impact of Satan's schemes at one time or another.

The sound was especially familiar to me, because I had just walked through a difficult time in ministry. A time marked by painful misunderstandings and feelings of deep betrayal. I knew what it felt like to be closed off and hemmed in, shut inside my tomb.

But later that night, as I looked at the box sitting in my hotel room, I suddenly realized something else.

A part of me *liked* the grave.

I felt safe there, surrounded by walls of self-pity. The lid of offense promised to close me off from everything that had caused me pain. Though I'd battled to forgive and move on, I still had moments when I preferred the shelter of the tomb to the full light of day.

Dethroning Lies

Many of us believe the lie that we are helpless when it comes to finding true freedom. Our bondage seems too strong and the lies too intense. Yet regularly employing these four powerful principles releases the Holy Spirit to release *us*:

Reveal. Ask God to show the area (or areas) in which you are bound. What stronghold is preventing you from experiencing freedom? What lie has exalted itself above the knowledge of God? Don't try to figure this out on your own. Ask for the Spirit's help.

Repent. Ask God to forgive the times you've sought refuge in your stronghold rather than in Him. Ask the Holy Spirit to take your sin and the accompanying lies and remove them from you "as far as the east is from the west" (Psalm 103:12).

Renounce. Prayerfully renounce any authority you may have given to Satan by embracing your stronghold rather than God. Naming

For that's what makes tombs so attractive. They shut out what we don't want to deal with. They insulate and isolate us from pain.

Or so we think.

And so the Deceiver promises, fooling us into believing that our sepulchers offer two vitally important things we cannot live without:

1. *Identity*—an address that defines who we are and what has happened to us

2. *Security*—a sense of protection from outside forces

What nonsense! Any identity or security we might find inside our strongholds is an illusion—and a dangerous one at that. Though it may be frightening to think

each sin aloud, renounce your attachment to the lie or behavior, giving authority in that area back to Jesus Christ.

Replace. Look for scriptures that pertain to your stronghold or the lie you've believed. Write them down and place them where you can read them several times a day. Memorize and quote these verses whenever you feel the lie trying to reassert its power.

Please note that I'm not outlining four easy steps for curing your hurts, hang-ups, and habits. Strongholds may have a physical or spiritual component, so the process of breaking free can be lengthy and complicated. Some (especially addictions) may require significant time to overcome as well as outside help, such as professional counseling, support groups, intercessory prayer, and more.

> *The weapons we fight with are not the weapons of the world.*
> *On the contrary, they have divine power to demolish strongholds.*
>
> 2 CORINTHIANS 10:4

about living outside our tombs, if we want the freedom Jesus offers, that's a chance we have to take.

Which brings us back to where we started in this chapter.

To the story of a demon-possessed man living in a graveyard.

What Jesus Can Do with Our Tombs

Aren't you glad Jesus isn't threatened by our tombs? In fact, He seems to go out of His way to find them. Which is exactly what happened when He left the multitude standing on Galilee's shore. After getting in a boat, He and His disciples began crossing the lake that separated them from a man in desperate need.

On the way they encountered a violent storm that threatened their lives. (Isn't it interesting how all hell tries to break loose just before some of God's greatest breakthroughs?) But the same power that calmed the storm would soon calm a tormented man.

Look at what happened when Jesus stepped ashore, for the encounter that followed can teach us a few things about what God is able to do when we give Him access to our tomb-dwelling lives.

The first thing we learn from the gospel account is that the demon-possessed man actually ran out to meet Jesus and "fell at his feet" (Luke 8:28). Though the demons inside him must have been screaming at the man to run away from the Son of God, he still went toward Him. Which is good news indeed. It tells us that while the enemy of our souls may do his best to separate us from Jesus, he is helpless to keep us away if we choose to come.

In fact, we might conclude from this verse that when we bow to Christ, Satan is forced to bow as well. Don't you love it?

Second, this story smashes the myth that our tombs—the strongholds the devil uses to keep us bound—offer anything remotely like our true identity.

When Jesus asked the man, "What is your name?" (Luke 8:30), the demons were the first to speak up, identifying themselves rather than allowing the man to speak. It was as though the poor guy didn't exist.

Isn't that what happens with our strongholds? Somewhere in our bondage we cease being us and become only our problems. Defined solely by our hurts, hang-ups, and habits, we wear a grave marker like a nametag.

Adulterer! it shouts. *Glutton!* it gloats. *Abused and misused, betrayed and abandoned,* it declares.

But over the cacophony of condemning and demeaning voices, please hear what our heavenly Father says about you and about me. "Fear not, for I have redeemed you," says the Lord in Isaiah 43:1. "I have summoned you by *name;* you are mine."

In other words, don't listen to labels. Listen to your God. You are His child. He knows your name by heart: "I will not forget you! See, I have engraved you on the palms of my hands" (Isaiah 49:15–16).

It is not your sin but His love that marks and defines you in His eyes.

And it's not your tomb but the place that God has prepared for you in His heart that offers true security.

THE ULTIMATE SECURITY SYSTEM

"When you pass through the waters, I will be with you," the Lord promises in Isaiah 43:2, 5. "When you walk through the fire, you will not be burned.... Do not be afraid, for I am with you."

Now that's what I call protection! And that is what we find when we exchange our midchamber existence for a home in the heart of God. Though Satan may huff and puff and try to blow our lives down, he won't succeed. For we dwell "in the shelter of the Most High" God (Psalm 91:1).

According to the Gospels, the tormented man who ran to Jesus hadn't lived a normal life for a long time. Luke tells us he'd stopped wearing clothes and ran naked among the tombs. Mark writes that the man cut himself with stones, cried out day and night, and broke loose from every attempt to confine him with chains.

So much for Satan's brand of security system. Does that sound like safety to you? Of course it doesn't. And yet many of us buy the slick ads of the Enemy that tell us we're better off holing up in our dark, smelly graves rather than trusting God and coming out into the light. Some of us have gotten so used to tomb dwelling that we've gone to great lengths to make our midchambers plush and comfortable.

Installing sixty-inch plasma televisions and high-speed Internet so we can pretend we're not alone.

We can't imagine leaving our strongholds, much less demolishing them. But the longer we stay gravebound, the more stuck we become.

I've counseled enough hurting people to see firsthand the naked wandering and mental torment that happens when we love our tombs more than we desire our freedom. I've also seen the ineffectiveness of relying totally on human effort to chain and contain our pain. For our lower nature inevitably finds a way to overpower all attempts to constrain our self-destructive tendencies. Both our own attempts and those of others.

The truth is, we need more than restraint; we need a resurrection. Not more chains to control our lower natures. Not more lists of dos and don'ts to make us fit into society. Although they might subdue us for a while, what we really need is a true, from-the-top-of-our-heads-to-the-tips-of-our-toes transformation! And for that, we need Jesus. For "if the Son sets you free," John 8:36 promises, "you will be free indeed."

I love how Luke describes the results of the Lord's work that day in the graveyard. After He cast the evil spirits into a herd of suddenly suicidal pigs, people from all around came to see what had happened. They found the man, Luke 8:35 tells us, "sitting at Jesus' feet, dressed and in his right mind."

Isn't that beautiful? The naked, out-of-control man they'd once feared now sat calmly and peacefully at the feet of Jesus, fully clothed. No longer insane and without the slightest desire to continue hanging out with the dead. Wanting, instead, to follow Jesus all the days of his life (verse 38).

That's the kind of life change I want, the kind of identity and security I crave. I want to be so transformed by my Savior that my nakedness is clothed and my mind is made completely whole. I want my life to be a testimony and so filled with Jesus that I'm completely out of place among the tombs.

"Return home," Jesus told the man, "and tell how much God has done for you" (verse 39).

Which is exactly what the once-possessed, now-Christ-obsessed man did! He not only went to his own town but visited Decapolis as well (Mark 5:20), taking the good news of the gospel to a many-citied region of Gentiles far removed from the things of God.

An encounter with Jesus had transformed his tombstone into a standing stone of grace—like the memorial stones the people of Israel set up after crossing the Jordan River (Joshua 4:8–9). A visible witness to God's power to save, heal, and deliver.

That kind of witness can be mine, and yours as well, if we'll simply choose to run toward Jesus rather than holding back and hiding out in our tombs.

COME AND SEE

"Where have you laid him?" Jesus asked Martha and Mary through His tears (John 11:34).

"Come and see, Lord," they replied. Then together they went to Lazarus's tomb.

Oh how I wish we could grasp the immensity and emotion of this tender exchange and what it means for us today.

Where have you laid your pain? Jesus asks us tenderly. *Where do you keep all your shattered hopes and dreams? Where have you laid the part of you that died when you failed or were abandoned, forgotten, betrayed? Where are you entombed and enslaved, hemmed in, shut down, and closed off?*

Come and see, Lord.

That's the only response we need to give. Come and see.

With the invitation, Jesus steps down into our pain and gathers us in His arms. He doesn't chastise us for what we've gone through or insist we explain the death we now mourn. He holds us close and weeps over what sin and death have done to us, His beloved.

He doesn't look down on our wild-eyed nakedness, because Jesus understands. He has walked where we've walked, and He has felt what we've felt.

"For we do not have a high priest who is unable to sympathize with our weaknesses," Hebrews 4:15 tells us. We have a tender Savior with a heart big enough to handle our sorrow and gentle hands able to carry our pain. "A bruised reed he will not break," Matthew 12:20 promises, "and a smoldering wick he will not snuff out."

So we needn't hold back. We can run to Him as the man living among the tombs did. We needn't self-protect or weigh our words. We can be bold—even desperate like Mary and Martha—as we pour out our fear and disappointment before Him. "Come and see, Lord," we can say, knowing with full assurance that He will come and He will see.

And because of that, all hell trembles. Satan and his demons see what we don't see, and they know what we may not yet fully realize: The victory has already been won. The stone has been rolled away, and the tomb is empty—not only Christ's grave, but ours as well. For sin no longer has power over us (Romans 6:14, NKJV).

But we still have to decide where we will live. Will it be the familiarity of the graveyard or a new life in Christ, as scary as that may seem? Will we choose bondage, or will we choose freedom?

In a sense it's up to us. For the resurrection work has already been accomplished. "I am the living one," Jesus declares in Revelation 1:18. "I died, but look—I am alive forever and ever! And I hold the keys of death and the grave" (NLT).

Which means, of course, He has the ability to open your tomb and mine. Even now He stands outside the doors of our strongholds, our dark, lonely midchambers. Calling with a voice like tender thunder as He challenges you and me.

"Lazarus, come forth...and live!"

When Martha heard that Jesus was coming, she went out
to meet him, but Mary stayed at home.
"Lord," Martha said to Jesus, "if you had been here,
my brother would not have died.
But I know that even now God will give you whatever you ask."
Jesus said to her, "Your brother will rise again."
Martha answered, "I know he will rise again in
the resurrection at the last day."
Jesus said to her, "I am the resurrection and the life.
He who believes in me will live, even though he dies;
and whoever lives and believes in me will never die.
Do you believe this?"
"Yes, Lord," she told him. "I believe that you are the Christ,
the Son of God, who was to come into the world."….
Jesus, once more deeply moved, came to the tomb.
It was a cave with a stone laid across the entrance.
"Take away the stone," he said.
"But, Lord," said Martha, the sister of the dead man,
"by this time there is a bad odor, for he has been there four days."
Then Jesus said, "Did I not tell you that if you believed,
you would see the glory of God?"

JOHN 11:20–27, 38–40

Roll Away the Stone

I can only imagine what it must have been like. Standing there before the tomb, hoping for the best yet fearing the worst, Mary and Martha must have clasped hands and looked at each other with a mixture of fear and wonder.

"Take away the stone," Jesus had ordered (John 11:39). While Martha wanted to obey, her practicality couldn't help but point out a problem with the plan. "By this time there is a bad odor," she said. The King James Version puts it more bluntly: "He stinketh." After four days of Judean heat and the natural decay of the human body—well, opening the tomb didn't promise to be a pleasant experience.

Why would Jesus want to do that? she must have wondered. Perhaps He wanted to pay His last respects. Perhaps He wanted to see His dear friend one last time, even in death.

Earlier that day, when they'd talked on the road, He'd promised that her brother would rise again. But He didn't mean today, did He?

Right now?

But that is exactly what the Lord had in mind in verse 40. "Did I not tell you that if you believed, you would see the glory of God?" Jesus asked Martha, looking intently into her eyes. And in that moment a decision had to be made.

Would Martha obey Jesus?

Or was the risk of revealing what lay behind the stone too much to bear?

Our Part to Play

To obey or not to obey—that's the question we face continually in our Christian walk. Some days it's easy to comply, but other days it feels all but impossible. Especially when God asks us to do something that doesn't make sense to us.

Something like opening a tomb.

Jesus didn't have to wait for those standing around to obey. After all, He was (and is) God Almighty. With just a word He could have shattered the boulder that lay across Lazarus's grave. That would have been dramatic.

"Why not do an instantaneous miracle like that in my life, Lord?" we ask. "That's what I'd prefer."

Better yet, Jesus could have left the stone in place, and then—to really show His power—just waved His hand, and *poof!* Lazarus could have suddenly appeared, standing outside the tomb in brand-new robes, glowing with health. Now, that would have been impressive.

"Do that in me, God!" we cry.

But instead, Jesus left the job of removing the stone to those standing around Him. For the coming miracle hinged, at least partly, on the willingness of the grieving family to give Jesus access to their pain.

And that's true when it comes to our resurrections as well. While only Christ can make dead men live, only we can remove the obstacles that stand between us and our Savior.

All of us, you see, have blockages in our souls that we've allowed and perhaps even nurtured. False beliefs we've internalized as truth, to the point we believe them before we believe God. As a result, many of us have become, as Craig Groeschel puts it, Christian atheists—"believing in God but living as if He doesn't exist."[1]

I've identified three specific "boulders" that I believe many Christians struggle with. Three obstacles we must examine and relinquish so God can do the work He longs to do. For while Lazarus was powerless to roll away the stone that sealed his tomb, we are not. Our choices and attitudes really do make a difference in our ability to accept Christ's offer of freedom.

So what stones must be rolled away?

The first is the stone of unworthiness—the lie that we are unloved and unlovable.

The second is the stone of unforgiveness—the lie that we must hold on to the hurts of the past.

And the third is the stone of unbelief—the lie that God can't or won't help us so we must do everything ourselves.

Unworthiness, unforgiveness, unbelief—they're daunting, intimidating blockages that lock us in and cut us off. But not one of them is impossible to remove. Not when we put our shoulders to our boulders and cry out to God for help.

The Stone of Unworthiness

Remember my friend Lisa, whom you met in chapter 1? The vibrant Christian who stopped me after Bible study and confessed that she could tell other people Jesus loved them but couldn't convince herself she was accepted by God?

As she and I spent time together that day, we asked the Holy Spirit to reveal what was keeping her heart from truly receiving the good news of God's love. After our prayer Lisa began to tell me the story of her conversion—a beautiful story, indeed. But one thing haunted her, Lisa said. A secret she had told no one, not even her husband.

With tears running down her cheeks, she confessed her shame. "I had an abortion in high school. But not just one, Joanna. I had multiple abortions." Sobs shook my friend's body as the immensity of her words overwhelmed her.

"How could God ever forgive me?" she asked, finally voicing the fear-filled unworthiness that had entombed her for the majority of her life. "How could He ever love me after what I've done?"

I held my friend as she cried and poured out her grief—grief not only for her sin but also for the children she'd never known. Her sorrow was deep and heartrending to witness but also transformative. For both of us.

"Don't you know, Lisa?" I whispered against her hair as the revelation hit my heart. "Don't you know that's why Jesus had to come? That's why He had to die."

We've all sinned. We've all fallen short of what is best and good and right. We've all taken shortcuts of convenience, choosing to ignore God's law and invoking the consequences.

My goody-two-shoes past was and is just as dark and sin laced as Lisa's wild years. Her sins may have been outward, but my inward sins were just as damaging. My pride, my insecurity, my idolatry of other people's approval. The driving force to succeed and the need to be well thought of. All of it lay exposed before me that day, just as wrong as any other sin. Just as needful of a Savior.

"He doesn't forgive us because we deserve it," I told her as well as myself. "God forgives us because we so desperately need it."

And that is what makes the good news so very, very good. The price has been paid. We simply have to accept the gift Christ offers. Our sin may be worthy of punishment. It may even have resulted in a type of death—death of hope, death of confidence, death of any future happiness.

But Jesus took it all on the cross.

And in the process He broke the yardstick—the condemnation that has hung over our lives, declaring us unworthy.

His sacrifice has the power to roll away our shame if we will allow it. Because of Christ's death, we have been accepted into the ranks of the righteous. Our track record has nothing to do with it—we need to settle that fact forever. The only thing that saves us is the Cross and nothing but the Cross. We can't add to it, nor can we diminish it. We simply have to embrace it. And when we do, the stone of unworthiness rolls away.

It has been thrilling to watch Lisa resurrect! Though she'd repented of her sin years before, it wasn't until she revealed her secret to someone else, as frightening as that must have been, that she experienced a breakthrough in her relationship with the Lord.

Perhaps that's why the Holy Spirit inspired James, a brother of Jesus, to write, "Confess your sins to each other and pray for each other so that you may be healed" (James 5:16). While it didn't happen overnight, Lisa's healing has come. Today she shares her story with junior-high and high-school students, urging them to commit to sexual purity but also reminding them that there is forgiveness and a fresh start in Jesus Christ.

What once brought Lisa great shame is now being used by God to bring Him great glory. But it all started with a courageous decision to roll away her stone.

THE STONE OF UNFORGIVENESS

Lisa's boulder was a sense of personal unworthiness along with debilitating guilt and shame over what she had done. But for many of us, our spiritual blockages result from what has been done to us—and our attitudes about it. We've been hurt. We've been falsely accused or misunderstood, misused or betrayed. And we can't seem to get past our anger, resentment, or bitterness.

We *want* to forgive—well, most of the time. Trouble is, we aren't sure we can forgive. The hurt has gone so deep that the tendrils of our pain seem to go on forever. How do you let go of something that has such a hold on you?

That was my dilemma several years ago. "I have to get alone with God," I told my husband, John. "I'm in a very bad place."

As I mentioned in the last chapter, we'd walked through a trying time in ministry, and for the most part I'd handled it pretty well. Miraculously well, in fact. A space of grace had opened up for me to walk through the difficulty without feeling the intense need to fix it or change the people involved. (I told you it was miraculous.)

But somewhere near the anniversary of the hurt, I picked up an offense against someone in the situation. Pain-laced memories began to stick in my craw and bother me anew. Opportunities for self-pity had floated through my mind before, but up to that point I hadn't indulged them. Instead, I'd been experiencing the also-miraculous phenomenon of a disciplined mind.

I'd learned that just because a painful recollection came to memory, I didn't have to embrace it—a revolutionary discovery, let me tell you. Instead of nursing and rehearsing the past, with the Holy Spirit's help, I was learning to disperse it, refusing the offense entrance to my heart and, more important, denying it occupancy in my mind.

However, this particular memory had slipped in through a side entrance. At first it was so tiny I hardly noticed it. But as I allowed my hurt a platform to state its woes, it began to grow, and a boulder of unforgiveness began to move across my soul. As a result, almost without knowing it, I began to cut myself off from people—and not just those who had hurt me.

I wasn't rude or dismissive. But I found myself escaping church services as

Disciplining Your Mind

"The battlefield is the mind" when it comes to the Enemy's attempt to derail our Christianity. But the best defense has always been a good offense, so I'm learning to train my mind for battle by disciplining my thought life. I don't always succeed, but I'm far more effective in rolling away my stones when I practice the following disciplines:

1. **Take every thought captive** (2 Corinthians 10:5). Or, as Joyce Meyer puts it, "Think about what you are thinking about."[2] Try not to let your mind wander indiscriminately. Instead, consider where your thoughts could lead you. If the thought takes you away from God, cut it off. (You really can do this!) Consciously bring it to Jesus and leave it there.

2. **Resist vain imaginations** (Romans 1:21, KJV)—you know, those runaway loops of what if, if only, and woulda-coulda-shoulda. When you feel yourself getting caught up in a cycle of fear, worry, or regret, stop! Consciously rein in your imagination, and shift your focus to Christ as the source of your peace (Isaiah 26:3).

3. **Refuse to agree with the devil.** When thoughts of condemnation or fear come to mind, remind yourself that they are lies, that God is bigger than your biggest problem and stronger than your greatest weakness (Philippians 4:13), and that He's taken care of the Accuser's accusations once and for all (Revelation 12:10–11).

4. **Bless those who curse you** (Luke 6:26). If you carry a grudge in your heart, it will consume your mind. When resentment arises against someone, begin praying for, not against, that person. Ask

quickly as possible, glad to have a small child who needed my attention. Calls to have lunch with friends went unanswered. Conversations became more polite than personal as I withdrew into my safe little world. My dark little tomb.

God to bless and reveal Himself to him or her…and to help you move past your resentment. (It may take some time to actually *feel* forgiving!)

5. **Renew your mind with the Word of God** (Romans 12:2; Ephesians 5:26). Get into the Word daily, and allow it to transform your thinking. Find a scripture that speaks to your particular situation, then memorize it, making it part of your mental arsenal against the lies of the Enemy.

6. **Speak truth to yourself** (John 8:32). Too many of us play and replay demeaning self-talk and other negative ideas that are contrary to what God has said. Consciously counter that tendency by repeating God's truth to yourself. Declare what you know to be greater than what you feel, proclaiming what God says about you and His power to save.

7. **Develop an attitude of gratitude.** Purposefully think about things that are of "good report" (Philippians 4:8, KJV). Make a list if you need to. Don't give voice to negativity—inwardly or outwardly. Instead, declare out loud your thankfulness to God (1 Thessalonians 5:18).

And now, dear brothers and sisters, one final thing.
Fix your thoughts on what is true, and honorable, and right,
and pure, and lovely, and admirable.
Think about things that are excellent and worthy of praise.
PHILIPPIANS 4:8, NLT

Finally the chill of bitterness sank in so deep I couldn't find the "want to" to forgive. That terrified me.

And so, with John's blessing, I holed up in a friend's cabin and poured out my heart before the Lord. It was slow going at first. My emotions were rock hard, but as I hammered out obedience to forgiveness, the stone slowly began to roll away.

At the Spirit's prompting, I wrote a letter to the person who had hurt me. I didn't measure my words; I just spilled out my pain. It was difficult giving myself permission to vent, for fear I might never stop, but I knew I had to get honest before God about what I was feeling. After all, as someone once said, "Holding onto bitterness is like drinking poison and waiting for the other person to die."

Funny how pain tends to land on a single scapegoat. After laying down my hurt before the Lord, I was suddenly able to see there were other people I'd been holding in the dungeon of my disapproval. People I needed to write to as well.

None of the letters would ever be postmarked, however. I wasn't writing them for anyone but me. My friends may not have felt the stranglehold of my judgment, but I certainly had.

Letter after letter I allowed the toxic pain to drain from infected wounds, ending each note with a declaration of amnesty and love. I would not hold my hurt against them one more day. Finally I wrote a letter to God, relinquishing all rights to resentment and asking Him to bless the people involved.

I was absolutely exhausted when I penned the last note. But with the exhaustion came the beginning of a sweet sense of release.

For with the mind-over-emotion choice to forgive, my stone of unforgiveness started to move. And somewhere in letting go of those who had hurt me, I walked out free.

THE BIGGEST STONE OF ALL

Unworthiness—that's what Lisa wrestled with. The lie that she didn't deserve God's love.

Unforgiveness—that was my issue. The lie that people who had hurt me should be excluded from my love.

Both false beliefs can thwart our growth as Christians, because they prevent us from moving past our failure or pain. But the reason the stones appeared in the first place isn't the issue. What should concern us most is the fact that we don't live free.

Which brings me to the third stone: unbelief. In my mind it is the most destructive boulder of all, because it is the cornerstone on which the other two rest.

If we struggle to believe that what Jesus did on the cross was really enough to cancel our sins, we will battle with unworthiness.

If we continually doubt that God could ever bring anything good out of our terrible circumstances, we will hold on to unforgiveness as our only recourse.

But nothing is more detrimental to our spiritual lives than allowing the stone of unbelief to wedge itself between us and the heart of God. Causing us to believe the Accuser's lie that our Father is powerless to help us—or, worse, that He just doesn't care.

I appreciate the honesty with which my friend Ann Spangler writes of her struggle to truly believe in the love of God. In *The Tender Words of God,* she details her journey to find her place in His heart.

> I have never found it easy to believe in God's love for me, except perhaps in the first days and weeks of my conversion. No matter where I turned in those bright days I found evidence of God's gracious care and steady forgiveness. The stern-browed god of my youth had suddenly and unexpectedly receded, and in his place came Jesus, bearing gifts of love and peace. Nearly every prayer in those days was answered, sometimes wondrously. I remember thinking that the problem with many people was that they expected so little from a God who was prepared to give so much.
>
> But years passed and something happened. It wasn't one thing but many.... It was tests of faith, sometimes passed and sometimes not. It was sins accruing. It was spiritual skirmishes and full-out battles. It was disappointments and difficulties and circumstances beyond comprehending. All these heaped together like a great black mound, casting a shadow over my sense that God still loved me, still cared for me as tenderly as when he had first wooed me and won my heart.[3]

In an attempt to recapture that sense of God's love, Ann went back to the only place that can set our souls at ease—the promises of the Bible—but even then she found herself unable to shake off her love-doubt. "Like many people who tend to be self-critical," she writes, "I find it easier to absorb the harsher sounding passages in the Bible than those that speak of God's compassion. Somehow, the tender words seem to roll right off me, much like water that beads up and rolls off a well-waxed automobile."[4]

But Ann persisted. Over the next year she immersed herself in the Word of God, allowing truth to wash over her until it finally began to stick, until God's love stopped being a concept and started to feel like a reality. It didn't happen immediately, but it did happen, especially when she began to exercise her faith rather than depend solely on her feelings. (See Appendix D: "Who I Am in Christ.")

But the real change came when Ann began to apply something she'd learned in a conversation with her friend Joan. When she'd asked Joan how she finally became convinced of God's love, Ann had expected a dramatic story—something about how God had spared her friend from tragedy or brought her through a dark time. Instead, Joan described a simple decision "to set aside one month in which to act as though God loved her." All that month "whenever she was tempted to doubt his love, she simply shifted her thoughts and then put the full force of her mind behind believing that God loved her. And that settled it for her—for good."[5]

Act as though God loves you.

Put the *full force of your mind* behind your faith.

Roll aside the stone of unbelief by *replacing lies* with God's eternal truth.

What powerful concepts—concepts that echo throughout the Old Testament and the New.

"Put your hope in God," the psalmist reminds himself not once but three times when he reflects on his troubles and grows disheartened (Psalms 42:5, 11; 43:5).

"Set your mind on things above, not on earthly things," Paul advises the Colossian believers faced with a new age philosophy that sought to undermine the purity of their doctrine (Colossians 3:2).

"We live by faith, not by sight," Paul adds in 2 Corinthians 5:7, still choosing to believe God though he was in prison and under threat of death.

Over and over, the Bible urges us to engage mind, will, and emotions in the pursuit of truths beyond our human senses. For when we choose to trust God above what we see or what we feel, we roll away the stone of unbelief and discover what real life can be.

Because faith does more than release our imprisoned hearts.

It releases God to work as well.

THE PROBLEM OF UNBELIEF

One of the most disturbing passages in Scripture is Mark 6:5–6. When Jesus returned to Nazareth, the people there were less than welcoming to the hometown boy. They couldn't wrap their minds around the idea that God might use someone so ordinary, someone they'd known from childhood. Sure, Jesus preached well, and they'd heard about His miracles, but rather than being impressed, they were offended.

"They could not explain Him," Kenneth Wuest writes, "so they rejected Him."[6]

As a result, the gospel of Mark tells us, "He could not do any miracles there, except lay his hands on a few sick people and heal them" (verse 5). Notice that it says, "he *could not* do any miracles there." Something held back His power. Jesus was limited by their disdain but even more by their determined unbelief.

Isn't it frightening to think that the people who should know Christ best often trust Him the least? And that, according to these verses, a lack of trust can actually limit God's work in our lives?

Oh how I want my faith to serve as a springboard for the miraculous. While my faith isn't perfect, I want to grow. I don't want to hinder God's work in my life or in the lives of those around me.

"Everything is possible for him who believes," Jesus told the desperate father of a demon-possessed boy. "Immediately the boy's father exclaimed, 'I do believe; help me overcome my unbelief!' " (Mark 9:23–24). Though small and underdeveloped, the man's faith was apparently enough. Jesus spoke the words and did what only He could do: heal the man's son and set him free.

Just as He wants to do for you and for me.

WRESTLING WITH SILENCE

Editors say it's best that authors don't include too much about the writing process of a book. I understand their point. I'd rather read a well-polished work than hear an author whine about how hard it was to pen. And yet for some reason my whining—I mean, my writing process—has made it into most of my books. Suffice it to say, I don't find writing easy. In fact, it's the hardest thing I do.

You'd think it would get simpler over time. I certainly hoped it would. But instead, each book has offered a fresh set of difficulties.

Writing *Having a Mary Heart in a Martha World* involved a yearlong bout with insomnia and living twenty-four hours a day in a wind tunnel filled with words and ideas.

Having a Mary Spirit was like wrestling a beast. The idea of cooperating with sanctification was such a huge topic it was all I could do to get my arms around the message, let alone fully grasp it in my heart.

But *Lazarus Awakening* has been completely different. Writing it has felt more like trying to hold on to water or to grasp fine sand—the concepts have seemed so ethereal and shifting. But even worse has been the disturbing quietness of my mind. For months on end I've felt entombed, locked down, and shut up without a breath of an idea to assure me that this book would ever live.

When I missed my book deadline six months into the contract, I had the bare tracings of three chapters. It was a far cry from the ten I'd promised to deliver.

"I feel like I'm holding a pregnancy test stick, and it says I'm expecting a book," I told my publisher, "but I have absolutely no symptoms. No movement, not even a tummy bump to tell me it will be born."

The only assurance I felt was that this book was God's idea and not my own. Though the echoes were distant, the bell that had sounded in my soul years before still reverberated. More important, I could hear God challenging me to believe, no matter what the situation looked like.

So it appears impossible? I felt the Holy Spirit whisper to my spirit. *So it looks like you'll never finish this project?*

"Did I not tell you that if you believed, you would see the glory of God?" Jesus asked Martha at the door of her brother's tomb (John 11:40). Standing at the threshold of my impossibility, I've heard that same question every day for the past twenty-four months.

Four days is a long time to wait for a resurrection. Two years feels like an eternity to write a book.

But if you'll believe, Joanna, you will see.

"Lean not on your own understanding," Proverbs 3:5–6 reminds us. "In all your ways acknowledge Him, and He shall direct your paths" (NKJV).

Don't look at how far you have to go, God seems to whisper each day as I sit down to write. *Instead, look for Me on the journey. Acknowledge My presence even in the middle of this emptiness. Don't try to work up faith for the outcome. Just believe in Me. Then you will see.*

So that's what I've attempted to do. Right here, right now, just barely past the middle of the book. Exercising my faith rather than giving in to my fear. And I'm finally putting words on a page—something that at times has felt literally impossible.

While the fear of failure is never far away, I'm determined to "contend earnestly for the faith" (Jude 3, NKJV). And while my confidence in myself wavers regularly, I will not "cast away [my] confidence" in Him (Hebrews 10:35, NKJV).

For greater is He that is in me than me that is in me (1 John 4:4, Weaver paraphrase).

And so with Martha and that little boy's father and everyone else who has ever struggled to believe in the face of overwhelming odds, I cry:

"Lord, I do believe! Help me overcome my unbelief."

CLEARING AWAY THE BLOCKAGES

I don't think any of us set out deliberately to block ourselves off with stones of unworthiness, unforgiveness, and/or unbelief. But life is hard, and boulders often roll across the doors of our hearts unnoticed, gradually and imperceptibly cutting off the light. Other times they crash down suddenly, unexpected and unasked for, like the landslide that blocked Montana Highway 93 many years ago.

I'll never forget reading about the incident in our local paper. After two years of heavy snowfall and successive wet springs, part of the hillside next to the highway suddenly gave way, scattering massive boulders across the road and shutting off both lanes of traffic.

Miraculously, no one was hurt. But it took crews several days, working around the clock, to open the road to travel. Which wasn't necessarily a big deal unless you happened to live or work on that side of Flathead Lake. For those who did, a detour was required. A two-hour, eighty-six-mile detour around the largest freshwater lake west of the Mississippi.

Faith That Rolls Away Stones

Jesus said, "If you have faith as small as a mustard seed, you can say to this mountain, 'Move'…and it will move. Nothing will be impossible for you" (Matthew 17:20). Imagine what that kind of faith could do when it comes to rolling away our stones! Not a faith in formulas or a faith in our faith, but a heart-focused trust in our God. I'm asking the Lord to help me overcome my unbelief and replace it with three powerful types of faith.

An *"even if"* kind of faith…
I want a Shadrach-Meshach-and-Abednego faith that refuses to bow to other gods or bend to the fear of other people's displeasure, even though refusing could result in death.

> If we are thrown into the blazing furnace, the God we serve is able to save us from it… But even if he does not, we want you to know, O king, that we will not serve your gods or worship the image of gold you have set up. (Daniel 3:17–18)

An *"even though"* kind of faith…
I want a faith that isn't dependent on circumstances or rattled by hardship—the kind of faith that chooses to praise even in the midst of unrelenting difficulties.

All because a pile of stones got in the way.

Tombstones. Roadblocks. What is barricading your life today? What's cutting you off, shutting you down, causing endless detours and chronic disconnects in the free flow of your relationship with God?

Perhaps it's time to get out the heavy equipment and, with the Holy Spirit's help, begin removing the blockage in your soul.

For Lisa, the lie of her unworthiness required the blasting cap of confession.

Even though the fig trees have no blossoms, and there are no grapes on the vines; even though the olive crop fails, and the fields lie empty and barren; even though the flocks die in the fields, and the cattle barns are empty, yet I will rejoice in the LORD! I will be joyful in the God of my salvation! (Habakkuk 3:17–18, NLT)

A *"nevertheless"* kind of faith...

I want the kind of faith Jesus displayed in the Garden of Gethsemane. A faith that says, "Here's what I'd like to happen..." but in the end wants what God wants most of all.

O My Father, if it is possible, let this cup pass from Me; nevertheless, not as I will, but as you will. (Matthew 26:39, NKJV)

And without faith it is impossible to
please God, because anyone who comes to him
must believe that he exists and that he rewards those
who earnestly seek him.
HEBREWS 11:6

Before she could live free, she had to reveal the dark secret that had kept her spiritually gagged and emotionally bound for most of her adult life.

For me, a jackhammer of forgiveness was needed to break the rock of resentment that had lodged against my heart. I had to face my pain but then relinquish my right to be offended so that I might choose instead to forgive.

For Ann, the rock of unbelief required a large dose of the *dunamis*—or dynamite[7]—of God's Word. Once she chose to exalt His truth over her feelings, the lie that she was unloved could finally be removed.

"Take away the stone," Jesus commanded those standing around Lazarus's tomb on that long-ago day in Bethany (John 11:39). Though Martha was clearly uncomfortable with the idea of rolling away the only thing that stood between her and the death she mourned, she chose to obey. Though she didn't fully understand why Jesus asked what He asked, she did what she could so Jesus could do the rest.

And in a sense, that's all Christ asks of you and me.

Roll away the stone, beloved. Do what only you can do. Choose to receive My love… choose to forgive…choose to trust in Me no matter what. Then watch what I will do.

For if you believe, our Savior promises, *then you will see…*

the glory of God released in your life and mine to bring us out of our tombs…

fully alive and completely set free.

After he had said this, he went on to tell them,
"Our friend Lazarus has fallen asleep;
but I am going there to wake him up."....
So they took away the stone. Then Jesus looked up and said,
"Father, I thank you that you have heard me.
I knew that you always hear me,
but I said this for the benefit of the people standing here,
that they may believe that you sent me."
When he had said this, Jesus called in a loud voice,
"Lazarus, come out!"

JOHN 11:11, 41–43

When Love Calls Your Name

I t's a long drive across Montana. Seven hundred miles, to be exact.

As a young wife and mother living on the very eastern edge of the state, I used to make the drive home to western Montana several times a year. Fastening my first-born in the backseat, I'd place John Michael where I could tickle his toes or hand him a toy for entertainment until he fell asleep. Then, hoping to make time pass more quickly, I'd turn on the radio. But just as towns are few and far between on Montana's eastern plains, so are the radio stations.

Instead of receiving a clear signal, I'd usually get lots of white noise—long strands of static broken now and then by fractured music as I passed over a station. Fortunately, the highway stretched straight and wide before me, so I could concentrate on slowly turning the radio dial, trying to home in on a signal. Until finally, out of all the static, a voice could be heard clear and strong.

I'm coming to believe that it takes that same kind of concentration to break though the white noise of this world and hear the voice of God. A purposeful tuning of our hearts to the voice of His Spirit.

For until we learn to truly listen, we may never hear Love call our name.

COME FORTH!

I wonder what it was like for Lazarus when he heard Jesus's voice from inside his tomb. Was it a far-off echo he first heard? A familiar yet distant voice calling him back from the holding cell of death?

I wonder what happened in Lazarus's body at the sound of his name. Did his heart suddenly start beating again? Was there a great intake of air as he drew his first breath in days? Did he awaken slowly, or did energy come like a lightning bolt, sitting him up straight before propelling him out of the tomb?

Either way, once he was fully conscious, Lazarus was faced with a choice. Just as we are. To go back to sleep and remain where he was or to get up from the grave and walk out into new life.

Because when Love calls our name, we can ignore His voice, or we can respond. We can pull back into the dark familiarity of what we've known, or we can step out into the light, tentatively perhaps and with eyes blinking to adjust, but ready to embrace what God has waiting for us. Though His voice may seem faint and distant, He is calling us out of our tombs just as surely as He called Lazarus.

So what should we do when we hear Him speak?

Only one response has helped me, and I offer it to you as well: choose to move closer. Answer His cry with your own. Shuffle toward the light, and you'll find the Light becoming brighter. His voice growing louder. His words becoming clearer.

All because you've chosen to listen and respond, tuning your heart[1] to the voice of your Savior.

LEARNING TO LISTEN

I remember being offended as a young adult Christian when people talked about hearing the voice of God. "God told me this…," they'd say, or "God told me that…"

"Oh yeah?" I wanted to respond. "Just who do you think you are? How do you *know* that was God talking and not a figment of your imagination? Or the guacamole you just ate?"

After all, I was a twenty-eight-year-old pastor's wife. I'd been raised in the church and had loved Jesus since I was a little girl. But I'd never actually heard God's voice—or so I thought.

I've come to realize, however, that although I have yet to hear God speak audibly, it would be untrue to say I haven't heard His voice. In fact, I believe the Lord is speaking to me more often than I know. The problem is, I'm not always listening. And when I do, the Enemy does his best to convince me that what I'm hearing is anything but the voice of God.

Priscilla Shirer describes this problem in her excellent book *Discerning the Voice of God:*

> If God wants us to hear His voice, the Father of Lies is going to do everything
> he can to make us think that we *aren't* hearing it. When we hear from God,
> we call it intuition, coincidence, or even luck—anything but what it is: the
> voice of God. We're so used to dismissing His voice that we've convinced
> ourselves that He no longer speaks to His children. But the Bible says over
> and over that God *does* speak to us. We *are* hearing from Him. We just may
> not know it's Him.[2]

Some people have come to the conclusion that God speaks only through the Bible. They say that to assume He speaks outside of holy writ is not only presumptuous but dangerous. I understand their concerns. After all, claiming to hear the voice of God has been the excuse for a lot of insanity and outright evil over the centuries—murderous crusades launched under Christian banners, mentally ill mothers drowning their children, and lunatic preachers poisoning their flocks, to mention just a few.

But to conclude from such instances of misuse and abuse that God *doesn't* speak today would be to miss a precious part of our walk with Him and a necessary key to our freedom.

For if we don't hear God speak, we won't be able to obey.

And if we don't obey, we'll never escape our tombs.

DISCERNING HIS VOICE

Have you ever wished God would speak a little louder? Or, better yet, that He would sit next to you with skin on so you could really hear what He said? Could you listen better then?

Don't be so sure!

In the Old Testament, God spoke so loudly at times that His voice made mountains shake and people tremble. But instead of drawing the children of Israel closer, His audible voice made them step back—back to the perceived safety of their tents and a more comfortable, arm's-length relationship with their God.

"Speak to us yourself and we will listen," the children of Israel told Moses in Exodus 20:19. "But do not have God speak to us or we will die."

Though Moses did his best to translate God's heart to the people, familiarity does tend to breed contempt. While they heard the voice of God and feared it, Philip Yancey writes, they also "soon learned to ignore it."[3] So completely, it seems, they hardly noticed when that Voice fell silent for more than four hundred years.

In the New Testament, God's voice sounded once again—first in a baby's cry and later through an altogether approachable man named Jesus Christ. His voice sounded like our own, but He spoke with an authority and wisdom never heard before. His voice could be tender and soft with children and adulterous women, demanding and hard with hypocrites and the spiritually proud. Yet even though

The Art of Listening

"Before we can hear God speaking through the everyday moments of our lives, our heart has to be prepared to listen," Ken Gire writes in his *Reflections on Your Life Journal*. "Which is more art than science. At least it has been that way for me." According to Gire, preparing our hearts in the "art of listening" involves several things:

> *First,* there must be a sense of anticipation that God wants to speak to us and that He *will* speak. This anticipation stems from the belief that God is love and that it is the nature of love to express itself. The form of that expression, though, is remarkably varied. Sometimes love is expressed through words. Other times it is expressed through pictures or gestures or a variety of other ways, often very subtle ways that only the beloved might recognize. That is the nature of intimate communication. It is clear to the beloved but often cryptic to everyone else.
>
> *Second,* there must be a humility of heart, for where we are willing to look and what we are willing to hear will largely determine how many

Jesus lived with us on earth, up close and personal, the very proximity that wooed us allowed us to crucify Him as well.

You see, history proves it isn't a louder voice we need. Nor is it a voice physically embodied and sitting beside us. What we need most is to learn how to listen. Perhaps that is why Jesus said over and over again—fourteen times in the New Testament:

"He who has ears, let him hear" (see, for example, Matthew 11:15).

FINDING EARS TO HEAR

How does this work? you may wonder. If God isn't going to speak audibly, and if He's not physically present as a human who speaks our language, how are we supposed to understand what He's saying? How do we *get* those ears to hear?

---

of those moments we will catch. This posture of the heart stems from a belief that words from God characteristically come swaddled in the most lowly of appearances, and that if we're not willing to stoop, we'll likely miss God among the stench of the stable and the sweetness of the straw.

Third, there must be a responsiveness to what is heard. A willingness to follow where we are being led, wherever that may be. A readiness to admit where we are wrong and to align ourselves with what is right and good and true. An eagerness to enter into the joy of the moment. Or into the sorrow of the moment, if that's the case. It is this responsiveness of the heart that makes us susceptible to the grace of the moment. And it is what prepares us to receive whatever grace is offered to us in the next.[4]

Go near to listen… Do not be quick with your mouth,
do not be hasty in your heart to utter anything before God.
God is in heaven and you are on earth, so let your words be few.
ECCLESIASTES 5:1–2

The disciples must have wondered the same thing when Jesus told them He was leaving to return to His Father. What would they do without the God-with-skin-on they'd experienced daily for the past three years? Without Jesus beside them, telling them what to do, how would they survive, let alone carry out the mission He'd given them to do?

But the Lord reassured them that He wouldn't leave them alone or stop communicating with them. "The Counselor, the Holy Spirit, whom the Father will send in my name, will teach you all things and will remind you of everything I have said to you" (John 14:26).

And that's exactly what happened ten days after Jesus ascended to heaven. The Spirit came, the fire fell, and the trembling, fearful people who had felt so lost after Jesus died were now suddenly filled with power (Acts 1–2). More important, they were filled with Christ Himself.

For Emmanuel—"God *with* us"—had sent the Holy Spirit to be "God *in* us." And nothing would ever be the same. Not for them. Not for you and me.

The Spirit of God now dwells in the heart of every believer. Filling us, if we'll allow Him, with everything we need for this life and the one to come. Leading and guiding us into all truth (John 16:13). Confirming that we are, indeed, children of God and deeply loved (Romans 8:15–16).

And, yes, speaking to us—though not always in the ways we might expect.

"Listen to your heart," Henri Nouwen writes. "It's there that Jesus speaks most intimately to you.… He doesn't shout. He doesn't thrust himself upon you. His voice is an unassuming voice, very nearly a whisper, the voice of a gentle love."[5]

It's a voice that's easy to grieve and, unfortunately, even easier to miss or dismiss—unless we listen intently and train our spiritual ears to hear.

TUNED IN TO LOVE

I wish I could outline "Ten Easy Steps to Hear God Speak—Guaranteed!" That would appeal to our human craving for formulas. But God's communication is far more individualized and intimate than anything a self-help bestseller could teach.

Our heavenly Father knows the best kind of communication flows out of relationship. Anything less is just an exchange of information. Since intimacy with us has always been God's goal, it makes sense that hearing His voice would be linked to that very thing. The better we get to know Him, in other words, the better we hear Him.

Perhaps that's one reason God keeps the voice of His Spirit quiet and subtle—so we'll lean in and listen carefully. And perhaps that's why He doesn't converse with us every moment of every day—so we'll treasure the times when He does.

For the Lord wants to accomplish more than just telling us where to go, what to do, and when to do it. He wants to take us by the hand and lead us out of our tombs. Wooing us out of our fear with His tender love. Calling us to higher purposes and deeper places in our walk with Him. All as we respond to His voice.

I'm no expert on hearing God speak. In many ways I'm still a learner. However, I truly believe God wants to draw close to me and speak truth tailored to my specific needs. But in order to have ears to hear, I must open my heart to His voice. And that happens best when I

- prayerfully invite Him into my everyday life,
- fill my heart and mind with His Word,
- remain alert to different ways He may speak to me,
- respond with obedience.

TUNING OUR HEARTS THROUGH PRAYER

If we "lack wisdom," James 1:5 tells us we should "ask God, who gives generously to all without finding fault." Instead of worrying about our problems, we should "in everything, by prayer and petition, with thanksgiving, present [our] requests to God" (Philippians 4:6).

What incredible invitations! We have a Father who longs to meet our needs. But even more, we have a God who truly listens to the cries of our hearts.

Standing outside Lazarus's tomb, Jesus prayed these amazing words: "Father, I thank you that you have heard me. I [know] that you always hear me" (John 11:41–42). We can pray with that same kind of faith—all because of what Jesus did on the cross (Matthew 27:51). We can come boldly into His presence, not just believing, but *knowing* that we too have a Father who hears our prayers and cares about our needs. Including our need to hear His voice.

Like Jesus, we initiate conversation with God through prayer. As I've learned to "practice the presence of God"—the well-known phrase used of Brother Lawrence[6]—inviting Jesus into my daily life each morning and conversing with Him as I go through my day, I've discovered a little more of what Paul must have meant when he said, "Pray without ceasing" (1 Thessalonians 5:17, NKJV).

I'd always thought that meant spending hours on my knees, but instead it has proven to be more like an ongoing conversation with a friend. Talking to the Lord as I drive down the road or wash the dishes. Commenting on the beauty He's created. Thanking Him for a house to call a home. Sharing my concerns as well as my joys. Just talking to my Savior on a daily, hourly, and even moment-by-moment basis. And all the while listening in case He wants to speak.

That kind of free-flowing, honest, heart-to-heart prayer has done more than anything else to open the door of my communication with God. But journaling my prayers during my regular quiet time has also been extremely helpful. For me, writing down what's on my heart helps me get a glimpse of His. Journaling seems to peel back all my facades so that I get honest before Him and with myself. I've also found that recording my prayer requests—and God's answers—helps me nurture a spirit of thankfulness. Because if I don't, by the time an answer comes, I've often forgotten what I asked for![7]

Sometimes, I must admit, the dialogue of prayer can feel a bit one-sided, consisting mostly of me pouring out my concerns. But I'm learning to take a little time to give God a chance to speak before I present my requests, because I want to pray according to His will and not mine. Afterward, I also attempt to still my heart and wait, listening for any wisdom He might want to give in response.

To be honest, the answers to my requests and the wisdom I need rarely come immediately but instead unfold over a period of time. And more often than not, they come from the Bible.

TUNING OUR HEARTS TO (AND THROUGH!) GOD'S WORD

"I have hidden your word in my heart that I might not sin against you," David wrote in Psalm 119:11. If we want to *know* and *do* God's will, there is no better place to go than to His Word. And if we want to hear Him speak, storing up the truth of what He has already said in Scripture is an important place to start.

When Jesus told the disciples He would send the Holy Spirit to "remind you of everything I have said to you" (John 14:26), He was speaking of the same work the Holy Spirit wants to do for us today. But how can He bring to remembrance things we have never learned?

Studying the Bible regularly, memorizing Scripture, and taking every opportunity to hear the Bible taught and preached—all have increased my spiritual vocabulary exponentially and have helped me better understand God's ways. They have also provided an invaluable knowledge base from which the Holy Spirit can draw when I have a specific problem or when God wants to address an issue in my life.

I can't tell you how often I've received guidance through a verse I once heard or memorized. Without my consciously seeking it, a "God thought" will pop into my head at just the right moment—clearly a word from the Lord. But God has also used the power of His Word to speak to me directly in my quiet time with life-changing, tomb-shattering results.

In my early years of parenting, for instance, I struggled with a stronghold of anger. There's nothing like having headstrong, stubborn three- and five-year-olds to bring out the headstrong stubbornness in a mom! I did my best to change my angry ways, but it just wasn't working. I couldn't seem to stop lashing out at my children. Even worse, I found myself rationalizing my behavior as common and almost expected.

But then one morning the Bible dismantled all my excuses as the Holy Spirit spoke clearly to me through James 1:20. "For the wrath of man," I read, "does not produce the righteousness of God" (NKJV).

I still remember sitting there, staring at the words as the Spirit spoke to my heart. *Your anger might scare your kids into behaving,* He gently whispered, *but it isn't accomplishing the righteousness God desires. Not in them. And definitely not in you.*

That rebuke was the beginning of my healing. As I allowed the Lord to chasten my heart so I could truly repent—truly hate my sin and turn from it—He began to rewire my soul.

Though it took some time, I can honestly say that anger in parenting is no longer a stronghold for me. I'm eternally grateful for that, because it's allowed me to relax and enjoy Josh, our little caboose. But also it's helping me parent my adult children more gracefully (I hope!) and with less need to control.

Tuning Our Hearts by Recognizing His Ways

While Scripture is the main way God speaks to me, it's not the only way. In fact, as I've grown in my walk with the Lord, I've been amazed at His creativity and the variety of experiences He uses to communicate with me. I'm learning to watch as well as listen for the following four methods the Spirit seems to often use:

- *Repeated themes.* Like every wise parent, God repeats Himself when we don't listen the first time![8] So I've learned to be on the lookout for similar messages on similar topics coming from different sources. If the same topic keeps coming up, God is usually trying to tell me something. (Around the time the Spirit revealed my problem with anger, I encountered two sermons, several articles, and a conversation among friends on the very same topic!)

- *Impressions.* This wisdom from the Spirit usually involves an inner urge or prodding to do something or to go a certain direction. Sometimes it's very specific—*Call your mother* or *Stop at that store.* To be honest, it's often tricky to tell whether the impulse is God's idea or my own. After I obey the nudge, however, I can often look back and see it really was from God.

- *Confirmations.* This clarification from the Holy Spirit is especially important when I'm uncertain whether I'm hearing God correctly— whether the impression I've felt or the theme I've sensed is really for me at that particular time. Sometimes corroboration comes through Scripture or from other people, but it can also come from a sense of settled peace.

- *Checks.* Sometimes instead of confirmation I may feel a check regarding certain decisions or actions. I can't always explain it, but something doesn't feel right in my spirit. There may be nothing obviously wrong with the action I'm contemplating, nothing that bothers my conscience, but I don't have peace about it. In those moments I remember my mother's words: "When in doubt, don't." Later I may (or may not) come to understand what the Spirit was warning against, but that isn't as important as the fact I've obeyed.

Regardless of which of these methods God uses to speak to us, it's important to remember that He will never go against His Word. Therefore, I check any communication I believe I've received from Him against the principles of Scripture. If it fails to measure up with the Bible, I must set it aside, no matter how genuinely I believe I've heard from God.

That is why it is so important that we know the Word—and not just in our heads. "The law of his God is in his heart," the psalmist writes. "His feet do not slip" (Psalm 37:31).

TUNING OUR HEARTS BY OBEYING HIS VOICE

"Pay close attention to what you hear," Jesus tells His followers in Mark 4:24–25. "The closer you listen, the more understanding you will be given—and you will receive even more. To those who listen to my teaching, more understanding will be given" (NLT).

In other words, if I want to hear from God, I must learn to respond to what He says. I can't expect the Holy Spirit to give me further instruction if I'm not willing to obey what He's already shared with me. Obedience opens the ears of my heart and invites further revelation (John 14:15–16). And the quicker I obey, the better. For delayed obedience is just disobedience camouflaged by a promise.

Disobedience in any form is a serious problem because it hardens the conscience—the pathway by which the Holy Spirit often speaks. Like ear wax, our sin can stop up our ears, muffling God's voice. Because our rebellion has distanced us from God, we no longer hear the voice behind us saying, " 'This is the way you should go,' whether to the right or to the left" (Isaiah 30:21, NLT). Instead, we find ourselves drifting farther down the path of compromise and sin. And that is a dangerous place to go.

For if we allow the radio dial of our heart to turn whichever way it wants, we'll end up with white noise and fractured bits of worldly wisdom instead of the sound counsel of God. Inevitably we'll end up way off course, which is why Proverbs 16:25 warns, "There is a way that seems right to a man, but in the end it leads to death."

But, praise God, we don't have to end up there! A change of mind, heart, and direction can be ours if we'll just stop what we're doing and truly confess our sins. Repenting of our apathy toward the things we know God has already said to us through His Word and in our spirits. Allowing the Father to cleanse our hearts and wash out our ears so we can once again hear His voice.

The gentle sound of our Shepherd calling, "Come, follow me."

Following His Voice

I used to worry a lot about not hearing God's voice. I was so afraid that when He did speak, I was somehow going to miss it. And scriptures like John 10 only added to my concern.

"My sheep listen to my voice," Jesus says in John 10:27. "I know them, and they follow me." Because I was convinced at the time that I didn't hear God speak, I had to wonder, was I really of His flock? Did I really belong to Him?

But I found the answer to those questions when I took another look at John 10:27. "*I know them,* and they follow me."

You see, it isn't my pursuit of relationship that enables me to hear the Lord. It isn't my diligence in prayer or journaling or Bible reading. It isn't my proficiency at picking up on impressions or the quickness with which I obey. Instead, it is the fact that Jesus loves me and keeps calling my name. I am His chosen lamb. I belong to Him. He's going to do whatever is necessary not only to get through to me but also to help me develop ears to hear. And, surprisingly, He's willing to use even my failures to help me draw closer to Him.

Priscilla Shirer puts it this way: "Do I sometimes make mistakes [in hearing God's voice]? I sure do! But that's how we become spiritually mature—by practicing listening to Him speak and obeying His instructions.... God graciously honors our heart's desire to obey even when we may be a little off base."9

The best kind of communication, remember, flows out of relationship. And relationships don't just happen. Intimacy must be nurtured and given time to grow. It's a gradual process.

In a sense, we learn to recognize God's voice the same way a child comes to know the voice of his mother. Nestled inside the womb for nine months, the child lives close to her heart in complete dependence. Then cradled near that same heart for years, he learns to discern her voice above all the rest.

Even in a crowded room filled with distractions and toys, my little Joshua knows when I call his name. And he comes running—well, most of the time.

Let's just say Josh is *learning* to come running.

Just as I am learning to respond to my Father's voice...even when He seems so far away.

The Voice of God in Circumstances

God never speaks to us in startling ways, but in ways that are easy to misunderstand, and we say, "I wonder if that is God's voice?" Isaiah said that the Lord spake to him "with a strong hand," that is, by the pressure of circumstances. Nothing touches our lives but it is God Himself speaking. Do we discern His hand or only mere occurrence?

Get into the habit of saying, "Speak, Lord," and life will become a romance. Every time circumstances press, say, "Speak, Lord"; make time to listen. Chastening is more than a means of discipline, it is meant to get me to the place of saying, "Speak, Lord." Recall the time when God did speak to you. Have you forgotten what He said? Was it Luke 11:13, or was it 1 Thessalonians 5:23? As we listen, our ear gets acute, and, like Jesus, we shall hear God all the time.[10]

—OSWALD CHAMBERS

This is what the LORD says—your Redeemer,

the Holy One of Israel:

"I am the LORD your God,

who teaches you what is best for you,

who directs you in the way you should go."

ISAIAH 48:17

Waiting to Hear

I wish I could say that my life with Christ is now one long uninterrupted conversation. To be honest, my spiritual reception just isn't that good yet. But it's getting there, praise God!

As I spend time in prayer, I develop the habit of conversing with the Lord. As I study His Word, I store up rich principles to be brought back to mind when I need them. And as I attend to the ways the Holy Spirit might want to speak, then obey what I sense He's saying, I'm becoming more attuned to His voice and more apt to hear when He calls.

I must tell you, however, there are times when the conversation still feels more like a monologue than a dialogue. Times when it feels as if my calls aren't getting through. As if there's bad cell-phone reception in heaven.

"Hello? Are you there, God?" I ask. "Can you hear me now?"

Sometimes those glitches in reception stretch out into long, painful periods of silence. Though I'm listening as intently as I can—or at least trying to—I just don't hear a thing.

I'm convinced there are times like that in every Christian's life. Times when Scripture seems to say nothing and all our attempts at prayerful communion seem to bounce off the ceiling and crash to the floor. Times when the darkness of difficulty not only deafens but also blinds us, leaving us to grope in the dark.

At times like these I've come to believe we must go back to what we know about God—not what we're presently experiencing. Because as a friend reminded me during a dark, quiet time of my own, "The teacher is always silent during a test."[11]

So often we equate God's voice with God's favor. When He is talking, we feel His love. When He is silent, we battle fear that we've disappointed Him, or we struggle with love-doubt, wondering if He really cares. It is always important, of course, to check our hearts and make sure sin isn't blocking our relationship. But sin isn't the only reason for silence. There may be more going on than we know.

I've found comfort in a little story I once read—a story about a woman who dreamed she saw three people praying. As they knelt, she watched Jesus draw near and approach the first figure, leaning over her tenderly, smiling and speaking "in accents of purest, sweetest music." Then He proceeded to the next figure and placed a gentle hand on her head and nodded with "loving approval." But what happened next perplexed the dreaming woman:

The third woman He passed almost abruptly without stopping for a word or glance. The woman in her dream said to herself, "How greatly He must love the first one, to the second He gave His approval, but none of the special demonstrations of love He gave the first; and the third must have grieved Him deeply, for He gave her no word at all and not even a passing look.

"I wonder what she has done, and why He made so much difference between them?" As she tried to account for the action of her Lord, He Himself stood by her and said: "O woman! how wrongly hast thou interpreted Me. The first kneeling woman needs all the weight of My tenderness and care to keep her feet in My narrow way. She needs My love, thought and help every moment of the day. Without it she would fail and fall.

"The second has stronger faith and deeper love, and I can trust her to trust Me however things may go and whatever people do.

"The third, whom I seemed not to notice, and even to neglect, has faith and love of the finest quality, and her I am training by quick and drastic processes for the highest and holiest service.

"She knows Me so intimately, and trusts Me so utterly, that she is independent of words or looks or any outward intimation of My approval… because she knows that I am working in her for eternity, and that what I do, though she knows not the explanation now, she will understand hereafter."[12]

Dear friend, don't be afraid of the times when Christ seems "silent in his love" (Zephaniah 3:17, DRA), when He answers "not a word" (Matthew 15:23, KJV). Because God is up to something more in your life and mine than just giving us the comfort of His voice.

He is working in us for eternity. He wants to be able to say of us, "She knows Me so well I can trust her with my silence."

As L. B. Cowman puts it, "The silences of Jesus are as eloquent as His speech and may be a sign, not of His disapproval, but of His approval and of a deep purpose of blessing for you."[13]

So in those times when God is quiet, trust Him and wait. For when the right time comes, you'll hear from Him again.

The very act of waiting, in fact, may help us tune in to His voice better than any other spiritual discipline. Because I've found that God often speaks in the middle of the night. When I'm quiet. When my heart's focused and my ears are ready to hear.

Driving across the dark highways of Montana late at night, I can pick up radio stations from all around the country. Spanish stations from Texas. Financial talk shows from New York. Obscure religious stations from who knows where.

So many voices. So many choices. But if I'll take the time to dial through all the noise, I'll find the one I seek.

Spiritually, that's true as well. For as I consistently tune my heart to the real thing, the counterfeits fade. Until all I hear is the Voice I need.

Love. Calling my name.

And I respond.

Now when He had said these things,
[Jesus] cried with a loud voice,
"Lazarus, come forth!"
And he who had died came out bound hand
and foot with graveclothes,
and his face was wrapped with a cloth.
Jesus said to them, "Loose him, and let him go."

JOHN 11:43–44, NKJV

Unwinding Graveclothes

Teacher, what must I do to inherit eternal life?" a religious expert asked Jesus one afternoon midway into His ministry (Luke 10:25). Not that the man really cared to hear the answer. He only asked the question to test Jesus. That happened a lot. The religious leaders in Jerusalem were frantic to discredit this upstart prophet from Galilee—the heretic they believed threatened everything they stood for, especially their position and power.

But rather than engaging in debate, Jesus turned the question back to the man. "What is written in the Law? How do you read it?" (verse 26).

I can picture the man gathering his scholarly robes around him as he began to quote scripture in a loud, pious voice. " 'Love the Lord your God with all your heart and with all your soul and with all your strength and with all your mind'; and, 'Love your neighbor as yourself' " (verse 27).

Jesus must have smiled at the man as He said, "You have answered correctly. Do this and you will live" (verse 28).

Not exactly the response the assigned troublemaker was expecting. Suddenly insecure, the expert volleyed back the first argument that came to mind, though it must have sounded weak even to his own ears. "And who is my neighbor?" he asked (verse 29).

In response, Jesus told a story that surely haunted the man and all who heard it, challenging them to go beyond the bigotry and hypocrisy that too often marked their religion.

Just as the story of the good Samaritan challenges Christ-followers today.

For this simple parable shatters many of the excuses and carefully formed arguments we Christians tend to use when attempting to escape God's call to a practical, yet radical, hands-on kind of love.

A Tale of an Unlikely Hero

You're probably familiar with the story. It's found in Luke 10:30–35.

> In reply Jesus said: "A man was going down from Jerusalem to Jericho, when he fell into the hands of robbers. They stripped him of his clothes, beat him and went away, leaving him half dead. A priest happened to be going down the same road, and when he saw the man, he passed by on the other side. So too, a Levite, when he came to the place and saw him, passed by on the other side. But a Samaritan, as he traveled, came where the man was; and when he saw him, he took pity on him. He went to him and bandaged his wounds, pouring on oil and wine. Then he put the man on his own donkey, took him to an inn and took care of him. The next day he took out two silver coins and gave them to the innkeeper. 'Look after him,' he said, 'and when I return, I will reimburse you for any extra expense you may have.' "

What was it about this parable that so unsettled the religious elite of Jesus's day? What is it about this story that captures the imagination of today's gospel-illiterate world?

Perhaps it is the insight into our own human condition that resonates most. For which one of us has not felt at some time stripped naked, beaten, and left for dead? Life is hard and habitually unfair. We can be minding our business one minute and lying comatose, barely breathing, the next. Crumpled at the side of the road in need of help, many of us have felt the cold shadow of indifference as people passed by, noting our condition but doing nothing to relieve it. We may even know what it's like to notice a problem yet feel unable to help. No wonder the story hits a nerve.

But I think what gives the story mythic proportions is its absolute unexpectedness. It highlights the compassion of an unlikely hero—a Samaritan, considered by the Jews of Jesus's day as the lowest of the low—against the heart-wrenching indifference of individuals who, by their very roles, should have cared the most.

"If you see your brother's donkey or his ox fallen on the road," Deuteronomy 22:4 commands, "do not ignore it. Help him get it to its feet." Certainly a wounded man deserved as much care as clumsy cattle. And yet in Jesus's story both the priest and the Levite—God's servants, entrusted with ministry to His people—passed by without stopping.

No doubt they had their reasons. They "were both in a hurry," suggests Henry M. Grout.

> They had been a month at Jerusalem, and were expected and wanted at home. Their wives and children were anxiously waiting for them. The sun would soon be down, and this was a lonely road even by daylight. Neither of them understood surgery, and could not bind up a wound to save their lives. Moreover, the poor man, already half dead, would be quite dead in an hour or two, and it was a pity to waste time on a hopeless case. The robbers, too, might be back again. Then, the man might die, and the person found near the body be charged with murder.[1]

Legitimate excuses, every one. But as David O. Mears reminds us: "It is not always *convenient* to be good."[2] Especially when it runs counter to our self-centeredness.

Inconvenient love—that's what we're called to as Christians. To "carry each other's burdens," as Galatians 6:2 tells us, for "in this way you will fulfill the law of Christ."

But such love is rarely easy. In fact, it can be downright messy. Especially when God asks us to unwind graveclothes.

Loose Him, Let Him Go!

I can't imagine what it must have been like to see Lazarus shuffle out of the darkness of the tomb, wrapped in thin strips of linen according to the custom of the day. His

Kissing Frogs

Transformation has always been the stuff of fairy tales—Cinderella's rags turning into a glistening gown and Beauty's love unlocking the Beast's curse. However, no fairy tale compares to the life-changing love story Jesus longs to live out with us. Strangely, while we are part of that story, we are also called to help write it. Wes Seeliger puts it so well, using a familiar tale to describe the important "unwrapping" work Christ-followers are called to share:

> Ever feel like a frog? Frogs feel slow, low, ugly, puffy, drooped, pooped. I know. One told me. The frog feeling comes when you want to be bright but feel dumb, when you want to share but are selfish, when you want to be thankful but feel resentment, when you want to be great but are small, when you want to care but are indifferent.
>
> Yes, at one time or another each of us has found himself on a lily pad floating down the great river of life. Frightened and disgusted, we're too froggish to budge. Once upon a time there was a frog. But he really wasn't a frog. He was a prince who looked and felt like a frog. A wicked witch had cast a spell on him. Only the kiss of a beautiful maiden could save him. But since when do cute chicks kiss frogs? So there he sat, unkissed prince in frog form. But miracles happen. One day a beautiful maiden grabbed him up and gave him a big smack. Crash! Boom! Zap!! There he was, a handsome prince. And you know the rest. They lived happily ever after. So what is the task of the [Christian]? To kiss frogs, of course.[3]

Be completely humble and gentle; be patient,
bearing with one another in love.

EPHESIANS 4:2

arms and legs were probably wrapped individually, which would have allowed some movement. But to say the man was restricted would be an understatement.

The stench of death surely lingered around him. Depending on the original sickness, bloody patches may have marked the burial garment here and there, interspersed with yellow-crusted infection. Though a welcome sight to those who loved him, the resurrected Lazarus might also have been a bit frightening to behold.

I wonder what Mary and Martha thought when Jesus said, "Loose him, and let him go" (John 11:44, NKJV). As happy as I'd be to see my brother alive, I wouldn't want to touch the strips of linen that had clung to his rotting flesh. After all, who knew what lay underneath the bandages? Just how resurrected was he?

Unwinding graveclothes. It's a dirty job. But someone has to do it.

Someone has to do it. And that's one of the factors of Lazarus's story that shocks me most. For while Jesus Christ did what only He could do—bring a dead man back to life—He invited those who stood around watching to help with the process.

"Loose him, and let him go." It's the same command Christ gives the church today.

I love what Jerry Goebel says about this passage of Scripture. "The work of Jesus is to bring life; the work of the congregation is to unbind people from the trappings of death. The words that Christ speaks are so full; he literally tells the 'congregation'; 'Destroy what holds him down. Send him forth free.' "[4]

Unfortunately, most of us would rather observe a resurrection than actually participate in one. Like the priest and Levite who passed by the wounded man, we shy away from actually getting involved in the work of loving someone back to life. Some of us may even prefer the role of cynic, refusing to believe that God has really changed a person or that the change can last.

"All too often, we never unbind those who Christ has resurrected," Goebel says. "We would rather continue to see them with the haughty eyes of the skeptic. We are more excited for them to fail than to change…[saying of their experience], 'Oh yea, well. I know that feeling and it will only last a month.' "[5]

An attitude like that breaks God's heart. And it can actually add another layer of graveclothes to someone who is trying to walk out of the tomb of his or her past. Goebel writes:

We bind people through our attitudes toward them. We bind them when we hold onto their faults instead of lifting up and encouraging their attempts to change. We bind people when we don't forgive them. We bind them when we gossip to others about their faults. Whenever we treat people out of our smallness instead of the Lord's abundance; we keep them bound.

We free them when we are determined to see new life in them. We free them when we praise God. We free them when we forgive them. We free them when we smile and welcome them, saying; "I am so glad you are here; do you have anyone to sit with today?" We free them the most when we seek them in their tombs and, "snorting at death," we command them in the name of Christ to come into new life.

Whenever we treat another out of Christ's greatness and not our smallness; we free them.[6]

That is the work we are called to as brothers and sisters in the Lord—unbinding, through acceptance and love, those whom Jesus has resurrected. However, as I've pointed out, helping people walk out into a new life can be a messy process. Though a person has received Christ as Savior, it may take a lot of time and effort before the outer self catches up with the inward work. None of us is born—or reborn—into this world squeaky clean.

Still, if God isn't threatened by the stink,[7] then why are we?

THE POWER OF LOVE

Unwrapping graveclothes—what an amazing call and privilege. But what does it look like, and how do we do it? Unfortunately, no template, no one-size-fits-all guide, is available. But having had the privilege of being raised by a man who loves Jesus so much that he's passionate about people knowing his Lord, I've had a front-row seat to quite a few resurrections.

One of my father's greatest joys has been ministering at the county jail for the past fifty years. Each Sunday he and a team from his church lead afternoon services for the men and women incarcerated there. Through singing songs and sharing the

Word and personal testimonies, they've witnessed some amazing acts of God in the lives of prisoners who've surrendered their hearts to Him.

However, Dad realized long ago that his responsibility didn't end with seeing someone saved. So he's done his best to disciple new converts, following up at times to the point of helping them find a job, a church, and a place to live after they're released from jail.

Once in a while during my growing-up years, that place was our basement. It wasn't unusual to have people stay with us for a few transitional days or weeks. My sister and I used to call our house "Gustafson's Home for Wayward Boys and Girls."

I suppose such hospitality would be considered too dangerous even to contemplate today. But back then? Well, it seemed almost miraculous.

Unwinding graveclothes—that's what Cliff and Annette Gustafson did on a regular basis. Mom's open arms spoke of acceptance, slowly loosening tight bands of rejection that had bound hearts for years. Dad's passion for the Lord and his commitment to family modeled a way of living some had never seen. It wasn't always a tidy process, but it was a valuable one. While many of the men and women Mom and Dad ministered to left and were never heard from again, others grew and flourished and still flourish today.

But the prisoners and ex-prisoners weren't the only ones who benefited from my parents' work. I did too. Watching them love in an active, hands-on way taught me several lessons that have proven invaluable in my own effort to serve the Lord by serving people.

What did I learn? First, that I'm not responsible for everyone, but I am responsible for the ones God lays upon my heart.

Most of the people Dad ministered to didn't stay in our home, but when he felt impressed to go the extra mile, he'd ask my mother for confirmation. If they were in agreement, they did what they felt God would have them do. Whether it was opening their home, lending their car, or investing financially in the life of another, whatever God asked them to do, they did to the best of their ability.

Second, I learned to lay down my expectations for the people I try to help.

The stories I observed in my parents' ministry didn't always have a happy ending—at least that we knew about. Most people were in and out of our lives within days. Sometimes my parents' generosity was misused or, worse, abused. A few "guests" became angry when my parents felt their job was through. If Mom and Dad had done what they did always expecting to be thanked or appreciated, they would have given up long ago.

Which brings us to the most important lesson I learned by watching these two unwind graveclothes: obey God and His promptings, then leave the outcome to Him.

After visiting the Missionaries of Charity in Calcutta, India, an American politician asked Mother Teresa how she could keep doing what she did without being discouraged. After all, the people the nuns cared for were so ill that the majority died within a few weeks. "God has not called me to be successful," Mother Teresa answered. "God has called me to be faithful."[8]

That is the calling my parents answered nearly fifty years ago—the same calling each of us has as Christians. To love the people He gives us. To minister to them just as we find them, gently peeling away their nasty rags and washing away the grime of the tomb with the truth of God's Word. Strip by strip, unwinding the lies that have shriveled their souls. Then covering their nakedness with our love and acceptance, just as Christ has covered ours.

For when we do it to the least of these, Jesus says, we do it unto Him (Matthew 25:40). Because Jesus loves people. Even people who are bound and still feel half-dead.

THE WALKING DEAD

My friend Sarah[9] knows a little of what it feels like to be resurrected yet still totter around in graveclothes. Her story reads like a soap opera and an exaggerated one at that—family problems, legal battles, loss, betrayal, you name it. When I first heard her tale, I thought that surely no one person could go through so much pain in such a short time. And yet she has.

As a result, Sarah has lived most of the last decade in a tomb of intense confusion and shame. Wrapped tight with sorrow over things she's done. Weighed down with false responsibility for sins committed by others.

When we first met, she had trouble meeting my eyes as we sat in the prayer room. Fearful of yet another betrayal of trust, she kept her head down as she tearfully told me her story. The pain was literally palpable as she spilled out the details of a life that seemed shattered beyond repair.

God had brought us together in a divine way—neither of us could deny that. It was time to step out of the tomb. Love was calling her name. But to unwrap the graveclothes? To open her heart and risk rejection? It terrified us both, I suppose.

As difficult as it was for Sarah to trust me with her story, I must admit I trembled as I listened to her pain. I know my inadequacies—my good intentions and lousy follow-through. What if I let her down? What if she went away more wounded than she came, her graveclothes wrapped even more tightly around her?

"Will I ever be okay again?" she finally asked, allowing her fearful eyes to glance at my face. I reached out and grabbed her hand, assuring her that we have a God who specializes in making all things new (Revelation 21:5). Then, together, she and I took all her confusion to the Lord in prayer. Laying out the story of her life before Jesus. Taking the hurt, the disappointment, and the betrayal to the One who has felt everything she's felt and more. Giving it to the only One who can heal a heart wounded beyond human remedy.

The healing hasn't happened quickly. Sarah would be the first one to tell you it has been a journey of stops and starts. One step forward out of the tomb, then suddenly, almost without warning, two steps back. One layer of graveclothes unwrapped, only to have the next layer pulled tighter. And yet there has been progress. True, measurable progress!

Helping unwrap Sarah's graveclothes has been a great privilege. But in the midst of this process, I'm reminded there are limits to what I am called to do. Because if I try to do more than God is asking, I could actually end up doing harm.

THE CHRYSALIS

In her devotional classic *Springs in the Valley*, Lettie B. Cowman tells the story of a naturalist who spotted a large butterfly fluttering frantically as if in distress. It appeared to be caught on something. The man reached down, took hold of its wings, and set it free. The butterfly flew only a few feet before falling to the ground, dead.

Under a magnifying glass in his lab, the naturalist discovered blood flowing from tiny veins in the lovely creature's wings. He realized that inadvertently he had interrupted something very important. The butterfly's frantic fluttering had really been an attempt to emerge from its chrysalis—a strength-building process designed by God. If allowed to struggle long enough, the butterfly would have come forth ready for long and wide flight. Early release, however, ended that beautiful dream.

So it is with God's children, Mrs. Cowman writes.

How the Father wishes for them wide ranges in experience and truth. He permits us to be fastened to some form of struggle. We would tear ourselves free. We cry out in our distress and sometimes think Him cruel that He does not release us. He permits us to flutter and flutter on. Struggle seems to be His program sometimes.[10]

Perhaps that is why Lazarus had to come out of the tomb of his own volition—why Jesus called him out instead of sending Martha and Mary inside to get him. Resurrection often seems to require a willing response, even a struggle, on the part of the one being resurrected. Tombs can be comfortable, remember. And choosing to live can be hard.

Those of us called to remove others' graveclothes need to understand that struggle. We also need to be clear about what our job actually is—and what it is not. We will be tempted to short-cut the time-consuming and painful-to-watch process of tearing loose from death. But if we insist on interrupting and interfering, no matter how good our intentions might be, we run the risk of derailing God's plan and spiritually handicapping those we're trying to help.

Overcoming the Fixer in Me

I learned an important truth early in ministry: There is only one Savior. And I am not He.

In fact, I do Christ a great disservice when I attempt to fill a role only He can fill. I also sabotage the process when I do things that the people being resurrected are meant to do.

Ministry can be heady stuff at times. It can be strangely satisfying to be the one a needy person turns to for help and answers. But it can also be dangerous...especially when we buy the lie that it's all up to us. That in some way we are meant to be another person's Messiah.

"If you become a necessity to a soul, you are out of God's order," Oswald Chambers writes.

> As a worker, your great responsibility is to be a friend of the Bridegroom...
> Instead of putting out a hand to prevent the throes [in a person's life], pray
> that they grow ten times stronger until there is no power on earth or in hell
> that can hold that soul away from Jesus Christ. Over and over again, we
> become amateur providences, we come in and prevent God; and say—"This
> and that must not be." Instead of proving friends of the Bridegroom, we put
> our sympathy in the way, and the soul will one day say—"That one was a
> thief, he stole my affections from Jesus, and I lost my vision of Him."[11]

Friends of the Bridegroom—that's what we are called to be. Loyal to Christ and His work in the lives of those we minister to rather than loyal to our opinions of how that work should be done.

For we will inevitably encounter moments when God's timing or methods seem a bit cruel, when situations He allows confound our understanding. But if we'll step back and give God room, we'll discover our Father really does know best.

Because God has always been more interested in shaping the character of His children than simply providing them comfort.

In setting people free rather than just letting them be.

And to that end He calls us to join Him in His work. But, surprisingly, we may do it best, not with our hands, but on our knees.

INVESTING IN FREEDOM

When the good Samaritan saw the wounded man lying beside the road, he not only reacted with compassion, he also did what he could do. He bound up the man's wounds, took him to an inn, and apparently spent the night caring for the stranger. Eventually, he had to leave the wounded man in the innkeeper's care—just as we must entrust the finishing work of healing in people's lives to God and God alone.

But that wasn't the end of the good Samaritan's involvement. Before going on his way, he invested in the invalid's continued care. Leaving money to pay for several days' lodging, the man from Samaria promised to return to settle any extra costs that might be incurred.

Oh how I want to display that kind of sacrificial love and tenacious follow-through when it comes to helping my brothers and sisters experience new life.

I want to see people set free. I'm tired of watching Christians walk out of church just as bound as they were when they walked in. I'm tired of seeing people struggle

---

Lessons from Good Sam

We all want to be used by God to help others. But we don't always know what that should look like. The story of the good Samaritan offers several lessons to help shape our response when we see someone in need:

1. *He not only saw but acted.* Other people passed by and saw the wounded man, but the good Samaritan was "moved" with compassion. He didn't just feel sorry for the man's condition; he *moved* to do something to alleviate his pain (Proverbs 3:27).

2. *He used his oil and his donkey.* Don't underestimate what your involvement can mean to someone in need. Investing your practical resources, your emotional support, and your precious time can make all the difference to a broken soul. A kind note, a warm meal, a listening ear—little is much when God is in it (James 2:16; Galatians 6:2).

3. *He went out of his way to help.* Initial compassion can wear off quickly, especially when helping others is inconvenient. The good Samaritan could have left the man at the inn and gone on his way, but instead he stuck around to do the hard stuff—washing

for years with the same issues, the same bondages and addictions, without realizing victory. I want to see people delivered. Don't you?

According to Scripture, such freedom usually involves a specific—and costly—commitment on my part and yours. For beyond our love and hands-on care, true life change and healing are nearly always preceded by an investment of prayer.

After nearly three decades of ministry, I'm coming to understand the best way to unwind other people's graveclothes is through intercession. But can I be honest? Prayer is often the last place I go. I'm ashamed to admit that I'm much quicker to get my hands on people than to get hold of heaven on people's behalf. No wonder I often end up doing too much or too little.

Reading Frank Peretti's book *Piercing the Darkness* has helped revolutionize how

---

wounds and staying beside him through a long, painful night (Galatians 6:9).

4. *He left the man in capable hands.* There will be times when a person's needs may be beyond our ability to help—times when a pastor, a godly counselor, or another professional will be required. Connecting needy people to other resources may be the most important thing we do (Proverbs 13:10).

5. *He promised to stay engaged in the process.* Following through to see how the person is doing is important—though at times God may ask us to do more. Whatever is required, never underestimate the importance of intercession—standing in the gap as Ezekiel did (Ezekiel 22:30), fighting for final victory in the lives of those we minister to.

The King will reply, "I tell you the truth, whatever you did for one of the least of these brothers of mine, you did for me."
MATTHEW 25:40

I view prayer. While it is a fictional account, it gives an important insight into the spiritual battle that rages around every single one of us. And it shows the vital role intercession plays in the spiritual realm.

You may wonder, as I have, if prayer really makes a difference. I love the picture Peretti paints in his riveting story. Though a heavy spiritual darkness lay like a thick cloud over the small town, each time a prayer went up, a small hole appeared in the darkness. More prayers, more holes allowing the light of truth and illumination of the Spirit to reach the hearts and minds of those living there.[12]

If we only realized how powerful and mighty our intercession can be, how it releases the power of God over people's lives and influences the spiritual battle being waged around them, we'd pray more.

In fact, I think we'd find ourselves investing in other people's freedom on a daily basis. Following through on our knees for as long as it takes for resurrection to happen and graveclothes to fall to the ground. Lifting people to the throne of grace until they're able to find their own way to the holy of holies. Covering them in the precious blood of Jesus until they learn how to walk and then how to run.

As James 5:16 tells us, the "fervent prayer of a righteous man availeth much" (KJV). Not only in the lives of those for whom we're praying, but in our lives as well. Because intercession tunes our hearts to the Spirit's leading, giving us eyes to see what He sees. And giving us His heart so that we can be His hands.

Unwinding graveclothes in the most unlikely ways and in the most unlikely places.

LED BY THE SPIRIT

Author Beth Moore tells of a time when she noticed an old man sitting in a wheelchair at a crowded airport. He was a strange sight, with stringy gray hair hanging down over his shoulders.

Trying not to stare, she focused on the Bible in her lap. But the more she tried to concentrate on the Word, the more she felt drawn to the old man.

"I had walked with God long enough to see the handwriting on the wall," Beth writes. "I've learned that when I begin to feel what God feels, something so contrary to my natural feelings, something dramatic is bound to happen. And it may be embarrassing."

Though she tried to resist the prompting, it only grew stronger. "I don't want you to witness to him," God said clearly. "I want you to brush his hair."

Finally she gave up arguing. She walked over to the man and knelt in front of him.

"Sir?" she asked. "May I have the pleasure of brushing your hair?"

He looked confused. "What'd you say?"

She blurted out her request once again, louder, and immediately felt every eye in the waiting area upon her and the old man. "If you really want to," he said.

With a hairbrush she found in his bag, Beth began gently brushing the old man's hair. It was clean, but tangled and matted. However, mothering two little girls had prepared her well for the task.

"A miraculous thing happened to me as I started brushing…," Beth remembers. "Everybody else in the room disappeared.… I know this sounds so strange but I've never felt that kind of love for another soul in my entire life. I believe with all my heart, I—for that few minutes—felt a portion of the very love of God. That He had overtaken my heart…like someone renting a room and making Himself at home for a short while."

The emotions were still strong when she finished. After replacing the brush in the man's bag, she knelt in front of his chair. "Sir, do you know Jesus?"

"Yes, I do," he said. "I've known Him since I married my bride. She wouldn't marry me until I got to know the Savior." He paused a moment. "You see, the problem is, I haven't seen my bride in months. I've had open-heart surgery, and she's been too ill to come see me. I was sitting here thinking to myself, *What a mess I must be for my bride.*"[13]

HIS HAND EXTENDED

What an amazing privilege it is to be the very hands of God in someone else's life.

I wonder how many opportunities I've missed. How many wounded strangers I've passed by because I was too busy to stop. How many piles of burial garments

I've avoided, not knowing that a resurrected sister or brother lay inside, struggling to get out. Or how many butterfly metamorphoses I've interrupted because my human compassion assumed that I knew the person's needs better than God did.

I want to participate in the miraculous. I want to be a little bit of God's kingdom come to earth—Christ's hand extended, reaching out in love. But that means I have to slow down, and like Beth Moore I have to listen. I must tune my heart to the prompting of the Holy Spirit so that when He beckons, "Loose him; let him go," I step forward rather than pull back. So that when He prompts, "Wait and pray," I'm willing to intercede rather than interfere. So that whatever I do, I do it with His wisdom and love. (For some practical help on unwinding graveclothes, see Appendix F.)

"Who's my neighbor?" the expert asked Jesus.

As Warren Wiersbe puts it, the answer has less to do with geography and more to do with opportunity.[14] Because the best way to love the Lord with all my heart, soul, mind, and strength is to love the people who happen to be standing next to me.

Even when loving them involves unwinding graveclothes.

Jesus said to [Martha], "I am the resurrection and the life.
He who believes in me will live, even though he dies;
and whoever lives and believes in me will never die.
Do you believe this?"
"Yes, Lord," she told him, "I believe that you are the Christ,
the Son of God, who was to come into the world."....
Jesus called in a loud voice, "Lazarus, come out!"
The dead man came out, his hands
and feet wrapped with strips of linen,
and a cloth around his face.
Jesus said to them, "Take off the grave clothes and let him go."
Therefore many of the Jews who...had seen
what Jesus did put their faith in him.
But some of them went to the Pharisees and told
them what Jesus had done.
Then the chief priests and the Pharisees called
a meeting of the Sanhedrin....
So from that day on they plotted to take his life....
[They] made plans to kill Lazarus as well,
for on account of him many of the Jews were going over to Jesus
and putting their faith in him.

JOHN 11:25–27, 43–47, 53; 12:10–11

Living Resurrected

I shouldn't have done it. Many months behind on this book's deadline, I needed to buckle down to make up lost time, but the invitation to speak at a church event in California stirred something in my heart. When they told me I could stay a few days afterward to write, I agreed to come.

I had no idea the location was Lazarusville.

The host church, birthed out of the 1970s Jesus movement, was filled with resurrection stories. Everywhere I turned, I met yet another person who had been spiritually dead and now lived again. My hostess had been a hippie traveling the highways of America when she encountered Jesus Christ in a powerful way. God told her to go back home and love her parents. She did. Not just in word but also in deed.

So drastic was the change in her that both of her parents accepted the Lord. "I gave birth to my daughter," her dear mama told me, eyes all alight, "and she gave birth to me!"

The event's worship leader, once a dancer and lounge singer, also encountered the amazing love of Christ and now leads thousands of people each week to the throne room of God. The husband of another leader, once full of bigotry toward Jews, now works tirelessly for the Lord, especially in the cause of preserving the nation of Israel.

One woman I met was brought to Jesus through her little boy. After years of looking for love in all the wrong places, Robin finally encountered the love of God through a memory verse her son had learned in Sunday school. "[Cast] all your care upon Him, for He cares for you," the little boy recited to his mother (1 Peter 5:7, NKJV).

"Who's 'Him'?" she asked sarcastically.

"Jesus, Mama," he said solemnly. "Jesus cares for you."

Those four little words broke something hard inside Robin. Though she was too proud to take her son to church that Sunday, she followed the bus and slipped in a side door. There she found the Love she'd been looking for her whole life.

Transformation. It was all around me that weekend. The sound of butterfly wings and souls metamorphosing in the presence of the Lord. Lazaruses and Lazarellas—every one of them.

None of them perfect. Not one of them complete.

But resurrected? Most definitely!

Undeniably so.

Before and After

When Lazarus came forth from the tomb at Jesus's call, those standing around couldn't deny that a miracle had taken place. After all, they'd just sat shivah—part of the traditional seven days of Jewish mourning—with Mary and Martha. They'd held the two sisters as they wept. They'd reheated casseroles, hoping to get the grieving women to eat. They'd even shared a few chuckles as they reminisced about their friend and talked about how they would miss him.

But now Lazarus stood before them alive again, his eyes shining as the burial cloth was lifted from his face. They heard his first words and witnessed his first steps after the graveclothes were fully unwound. They watched as the man they'd helped lay to rest now ran toward Jesus, along with his sisters, until they met together in one giant embrace.

Some of the crowd immediately put their faith in Jesus because of what had happened. Later, others would do the same. For seeing a man raised from the dead was hard to ignore. It was as undeniable as it was unexplainable. All they had to do was look at Lazarus to know a transformation had taken place.

He had been dead. Completely dead. Dead as a doornail.

Now he was alive. Completely alive. A walking, talking miracle.

No wonder so many who saw the event put their trust in the One who'd made it happen.

A Story to Share

I used to long for a powerful Lazarusville testimony. When you are saved at the age of four, there isn't a whole lot of "before" you can point to in order to validate your "after." Not a lot of transformation that people can ooh and ah about.

Over the years when preachers would say, "Think about the day you were saved and what you were before you met Jesus," I honestly wished I could. It would've been so nice to have a born-again moment I could point to and say, "That's where Jesus came. That was the old. Here's the new."

Dramatic testimonies seemed to be the ones God really used. Which bothered me a lot as a young Christian. What did I have to offer?

Sure, I loved Jesus. But had I been transformed?

Most days I couldn't see any noticeable difference between my life and the lives of those around me, at least from my hypercritical point of view.

I knew *something* had happened when Jesus came into my heart. After all, I didn't want to sin, and I hurt inside when I did. I felt a love in my heart for people and prayed diligently that my life would make a difference for God's kingdom. But I knew His kingdom needed to make a difference in me as well.

So began my lifelong prayer: *Lord, change me.*

And He has done just that. Although I still don't have a dramatic conversion story, every time I've allowed God to get His hands on me, He's given me a testimony—a real before-and-after story to share. Because every time I've given God access to yet another place in my heart, abdicating control and allowing Jesus to rule and reign, I've been changed in some important ways. While I'm not yet what I ought to be, I'm no longer what I was, thank God!

That's the kind of freshly baked, hot-out-of-the-oven testimony the Lord wants to give to every one of us. A testimony of resurrection that's just too good not to share.

The Resurrection and the Life

When Martha met Jesus on the road after her brother had died, a powerful exchange of truth occurred between the two of them.

After pouring out her pain and confusion concerning Lazarus's death, Martha gave Jesus permission to do what He thought best, by saying, "But I know that even now God will give you whatever you ask" (John 11:22).

In response, Jesus made one of His seven great "I Am" declarations, all recorded in the gospel of John. "I am the resurrection and the life," He told Martha. "He who believes in me will live, even though he dies; and whoever lives and believes in me will never die. Do you believe this?" (verses 25–26).

"Yes, Lord, I believe that you are the Christ, the Son of God, who was to come into the world," she replied (verse 27).

And Martha did believe! Unlike some of her fellow Jews, she had faith in an end-time resurrection. She knew her brother would live again, just as she would after she died. And she was also completely convinced her friend Jesus was the Messiah, the long-awaited hope of Israel.

In that faith-filled moment, Martha may have even believed He could speak resurrection life into her brother that very day.

But later, as Martha stood before Lazarus's tomb, her faith faltered. Face to face with her grief-filled reality, she found it difficult to believe that anyone—even Jesus—could bring life out of such obvious death and decay.

It can be just as hard for us to imagine such a transformation in our own lives today.

Yes, Lord, we know we're saved and going to heaven. We know that one day we'll be made truly alive when we see you face to face. But to think we might experience resurrection right here in the middle of our messy, mixed-up existence? *It just doesn't seem possible,* we decide, settling for the midchamber and just hanging on until Jesus comes.

Yet all the while, the Resurrection and the Life stands outside our tombs, calling our names.

"Lazarus…"

"Joanna…"

Put your name on His lips. Then listen as Jesus commands, "Come forth!"

But don't let resurrection be the end of your story. Allow Jesus to do all He desires to do in you—for He may have more in mind than you realize.

You see, Jesus Christ didn't come to earth simply to provide us an example to follow (though He did give us an important glimpse of how life should be lived). He didn't come only to show us the Father's heart and reveal the Father's love (though He did just that and more). He didn't even come for the sole purpose of setting us free from the tyranny of death (though, praise God, He did!).

No, Jesus came and died and rose again. Then He returned to heaven and sent His Holy Spirit for one reason and one reason alone: so that He might live His life within us. All of Him in all of you and me.

That's the testimony each of us can have, no matter what our faith journeys look like. The indwelling Christ living and working inside us. So transforming who and what we used to be that those around us can't help but see the miracle and put their faith in God.

It's the marvelous mystery Paul wrote about in Colossians 1:27—the secret "God has chosen to make known among the Gentiles" and to you and me as well.

What mystery? What secret?

Paul goes on to tell us: it is "Christ in you, the hope of glory."

THE VICTORIOUS SECRET

Over and over in the New Testament, we see this concept of the Lord living His life within us and transforming us from the inside out. The message is so pronounced, it's hard to believe many of us miss it. And yet all too often we do.

Hudson Taylor, the famous missionary to China, didn't understand it for a long time. After struggling to live a holy life in his own strength for more than fifteen years of ministry, he despaired of ever being victorious. But one day he read a letter from a friend, John McCarthy, who told of awakening to this marvelous truth:

> To let my loving Saviour work in me...is what I would live for by His grace. Abiding, not striving nor struggling; looking off unto Him; trusting Him for present power; trusting Him to subdue all inward corruption; resting in the love of an almighty Saviour.... Christ literally all seems to me now the power, the only power for service; the only ground for unchanging joy. May He lead us into the realization of His unfathomable fullness.[1]

But one sentence in the letter stood out among the rest. "But how to get faith strengthened?" his friend asked. "Not by striving after faith, but by resting on the Faithful One."[2]

When Hudson Taylor read those words, something deep within him responded. "I saw it all!" he later wrote to his sister, describing his new awareness of Christ living within. It was the Savior's faithfulness that mattered, not his own.

With that realization Scripture took on new life for him, especially John 15, which describes Jesus as the vine and believers as branches who draw life from the vine. Hudson wrote, "The vine now I see, is not the root merely, but all—root, stem, branches, twigs, leaves, flowers, fruit: and Jesus is not only that: He is soil and sunshine, air and showers, and ten thousand times more than we have ever dreamed, wished for, or needed."[3]

The reality of living and resting in the completed work of Jesus—the "exchanged life," as Hudson Taylor called it[4]—changed his life and ministry forever. A missionary friend wrote of the transformation: "He was a joyous man now, a bright, happy Christian. He had been a toiling, burdened one before, with latterly not much rest of soul. It was resting in Jesus now, and letting Him do the work—which makes all the difference!"[5]

But Hudson Taylor isn't the only Christian who discovered the beautiful mystery and magnificent power of "Christ in you, the hope of glory." Others have written of it as well.

In her book *The Unselfishness of God,* Hannah Whitall Smith writes:

What had come to me now was a discovery, and in no sense an attainment. I had not become a better woman than I was before, but I had found out that Christ was a better Savior than I had thought He was. I was not one bit more able to conquer my temptations than I had been in the past, but I had discovered that He was able and willing to conquer them for me. I had no more wisdom or righteousness of my own than I had ever had, but I had found out that He could really and actually be made unto me, as the Apostle declared He would be, wisdom, and righteousness, and sanctification, and redemption.[6]

Jesus wants to be the same for us today—living His life so fully within us that we join Hudson Taylor and Hannah Whitall Smith and the apostle Paul in proclaiming, "I have been crucified with Christ and I no longer live, but *Christ lives in me.* The life I live in the body, I live by faith in the Son of God, who loved me and gave himself for me" (Galatians 2:20, emphasis added).

Note that phrase "I have been crucified with Christ and I no longer live"—for it is the key. If we want to live resurrected and experience the exchanged life so many heroes of the faith describe, we must first get around to dying. Dying to ourselves until we're dead to the world.

For anything less than that results in a half-baked resurrection.

Don't Settle for Zombie Living

In his obscure 1906 novella, Leonid Andreyev paints a disturbing picture of Lazarus after being raised from the dead. Of the few portrayals of Lazarus in literature, this one certainly isn't flattering. Nor is it anything like the life Christ came to give. Here's a synopsis of the story:

> Sumptuously dressed, [Lazarus] is surrounded by his sisters Mary and Martha, other relatives, and friends celebrating his resurrection. His three days in the grave have left marks on his body; there is a bluish cast to his fingertips and face, and there are cracked and oozing blisters on his skin. The deterioration of his body has been interrupted, but the restoration, his return to health, is incomplete. His demeanor, too, has changed. He is no longer joyous, carefree, and laughing, as he was before death.[7]

Instead, Andreyev's Lazarus walks through life tormented—and tormenting those with whom he comes in contact. Looking too long in his eyes causes madness to the beholder. Rather than bringing life where he goes, a kind of death follows in his wake. He is a decomposing ghoul rather than a man made fully alive.

Sadly, I fear too many Christians accept this zombie-like existence as their fate. We're living resurrected—sort of. But we know our lives should be more joyful.

More peaceful. We know we should be loving, kind, forgiving. But instead, too often we're anxious, selfish, and cruel. The odor of our not-yet-decomposed lower nature seems to hang around our lives continually no matter how many disinfectants we try or room fresheners we plug in.

If you find yourself in this condition, may I ask you a question? Have you ever considered dying? Have you ever considered climbing upon the cross and staying there until Christ's life is able to have its way in you?

Though the Bible is clear that what Jesus did on Calvary was enough to purchase your salvation and mine, a sanctifying work still needs to be done—a holy transaction that requires a kind of death.

"If anyone would come after me," Jesus says in Mark 8:34, "he must deny himself and take up his cross and follow me." But may I submit that it isn't enough just to pick up the cross. We must allow the cross to have its way in us. Continually walking down the Via Dolorosa yet never allowing ourselves to reach Golgotha is not what Jesus meant when He said, "Follow me."

For without a crucifixion, there can be no resurrection.

We have to be willing to die if we want to really live.

Until we "put to death...whatever belongs to [our] earthly nature," as Colossians 3:5 commands, we will never be able to emerge from our tombs and actually "practice resurrection" as Wendell Berry describes it.[8]

Putting our earthly nature to death isn't something we can do apart from God. It isn't meant to be a renovation we attempt on our own or a charade we play at until it becomes reality. Believe me, I've tried it that way, and it just doesn't work.

And yet, while the Holy Spirit wants to help us, we must initiate the act. For in a very real sense, only we can choose to die.

PRACTICING RESURRECTION

The question, of course, is *how*. What does "dying to live" look like on a practical level?

For me, it involves rejecting the influence of anything that is in direct opposition to the rule and reign of Christ in my heart, including...

- my desire to control and direct my own life (and the lives of others),
- my right to be treated fairly at all times (and in all ways),
- my need to be well thought of (and thought of frequently),
- my insatiable appetite for escape (whether it be through food, television, books, or other avenues).

Did you notice that all these are me-centered desires? Which is exactly the problem. In order to facilitate Christ's life-changing invasion of the kingdoms in my heart, I must dethrone my lower nature by dying to self.

Buried in Baptism

To me, there is no better picture of dying to live than baptism. Perhaps that is why the first thing Jesus did before beginning His ministry was ask John to baptize Him (Matthew 3:13–17).

The act of baptism is practiced differently in various churches—some immerse, some pour, some sprinkle. However, I love the symbolism of the complete immersion we practice in my tradition. To us, going down into the waters of baptism symbolizes that we have chosen to die to ourselves, to our wishes and wants. Rising out of the water is a symbol that we have been resurrected to Christ. Our life is now His life. His desires are now ours.

As Romans 6:4 puts it, "We were therefore buried with him through baptism into death in order that, just as Christ was raised from the dead through the glory of the Father, we too may live a new life."

If you haven't been baptized, consider talking to your pastor or priest about following Jesus's example. It is an important part of confessing your allegiance "publicly here on earth" (Matthew 10:32, NLT), announcing to the world that you have died and Christ now lives in you.

Therefore go and make disciples of all nations, baptizing them in the name of the Father and of the Son and of the Holy Spirit.

MATTHEW 28:19

Or, to put it another way, I must crucify my Flesh Woman—that 683-pound sumo-wrestler chick I talk a lot about in *Having a Mary Spirit*.[9] She's what the New International Version refers to as my "sinful nature" (see Romans 7 and 8). And—get this—she thinks she's in charge.

Sadly, too often she *is* in charge. Though Jesus sits on the throne of my spirit, Flesh Woman still exerts a lot of influence in other areas. When I continually give in and let her have her way, her power increases, limiting God's ability to work in me.

For only I can decide whom I will serve.

"Don't you realize that you become the slave of whatever you choose to obey?" Paul writes in Romans 6:16 (NLT). "You can be a slave to sin, which leads to death, or you can choose to obey God, which leads to righteous living."

While I am not my sin, thank the Lord, only I decide whether or not I will be controlled by it. And only I decide whether Flesh Woman continues her tyrannical reign. That's why it's so important that I keep saying no to my self-centeredness.

And my tendency toward self-protection and self-pity.

And my natural inclination to be self-absorbed and self-promoting, self-actualizing and self-relying.

The list can go on and on. Just put *self* before nearly anything, and we've got a sin-sickness problem that can be cured only by a crucifixion.

But if we'll embrace the process of crucifying our flesh, we'll find the joy that Lazarus found. Because spiritually speaking, nothing frees us more than dying to live.

THE GREAT GIVEAWAY

Though there are many reasons to crucify our sinful natures, I think these may be the best: you can't tempt a dead person—or make one afraid.

Go ahead and try. Prop him up in a corner and parade beautiful women past him, and he won't even steal a glance. Set her on a throne and shower her with jewelry and fine clothes; she won't ask for a mirror. Threaten either one with a knife or a lawsuit, and you won't get a blink. Of all the millions of temptations and anxieties surrounding us today, not one can affect a dead man or woman.

That's why Paul, though faced with persecution and prison, beatings and even the threat of death, could say, "But none of these things move me" (Acts 20:24, NKJV).

How in the world was that possible?

I believe Paul remained unshaken and unmoved because he was already a dead man. He no longer belonged to himself. He no longer relied on *past* accomplishments or the *present* approval of men. Paul was motivated by a *future* hope that centered in Christ and being "found in Him" (Philippians 3:9). Everything else was just a big bag of "rubbish" (verse 8) to this man who had given up so much to give Jesus Christ his all.

That's why Paul could say with such confidence, "None of these things move me," then go on to say, "nor do I count my life dear to myself" (Acts 20:24, NKJV).

How dear is my life to me, I wonder. Too dear, I'm afraid. I tend to cling so tightly to my little life and its treasures that when the Lord tries to take away one of my precious toys, I fight to hold on. And all too often when He bids me come and die, I roll over and play possum.

Jesus didn't fight death. He embraced it, climbing onto the cross willingly. "No one can take my life from me," He said in John 10:18. "I sacrifice it voluntarily" (NLT). Oh that I would do the same. For on the other side of abandonment lies the freedom Paul discovered when he came to the end of himself.

The same kind of joyful freedom Lazarus must have experienced after he faced humanity's worst fear—death—and came out alive on the other side.

THAT'S THE LIFE!

Surely people must have found Lazarus different after his resurrection. Not different in the sense of Andreyev's zombie-like portrayal, but different in the sense of being fully alive and wholly unafraid.

When I think of the man, I imagine a joy-filled peace. A serene absence of fear. A holy carelessness concerning the things he used to worry about and the things he used to crave.

"None of these things moves me," I can almost hear him say.

Perhaps that is why people flocked to see this man, once dead but now alive

(John 12:9). But, unfortunately, what awakened faith in one awakened hatred in another—a hatred birthed in the pit of hell. For nothing is more threatening to the devil than a resurrected man or woman of God.

"So the chief priests made plans to kill Lazarus as well [as Jesus]," John tells us,

Unexplainable and Undeniable

In one of my all-time favorite books, *The Indwelling Life of Christ,* Major Ian Thomas explores the mystery and the power of living resurrected:

> The true Christian life can be explained only in terms of Jesus Christ, and if your life as a Christian can still be explained in terms of you—your personality, your willpower, your gifts, your talents, your money, your courage, your scholarship, your dedication, your sacrifice, or your anything—then although you may have the Christian life, you are not yet living it.
>
> If your life as a Christian can be explained in terms of you, what have you to offer to your neighbor next door? The way he lives his life can already be explained in terms of him, and as far as he is concerned, the only difference between him and you is that you happen to be "religious" while he is not. "Christianity" may be your hobby, but not his, and there is nothing about the way you practice it which strikes him as at all remarkable. There is nothing about you which leaves him guessing, and nothing commendable of which he does not feel himself equally capable without the inconvenience of becoming a Christian.
>
> Only when your quality of life baffles your neighbors are you likely to get their attention. It must become patently obvious to them that the kind of life you are living is not only commendable, but beyond all human explanation.[10]

When they saw the courage of Peter and John...they were astonished
and they took note that these men had been with Jesus.

Acts 4:13

"for on account of him many of the Jews were going over to Jesus and putting their faith in him" (12:10–11).

Wouldn't it be amazing to have a life like that? One that so glorifies God the only way to silence it is to kill it. A life that proclaims the reality of Jesus in a way that's neither harsh nor condemning but so winsomely alive and in love with the Savior that people can't help but want it. A life so filled with integrity and purity that critics struggle to find anything bad to say. A life that isn't shut down by threats of death or the fear of people's disfavor but simply walks forward in courage and joy.

That's the life I want. A life so dead to me and my old way of living that I can't help but live differently. The *exchanged life* on display for the world to see, no matter where I am and no matter where I go.

DYING DAY BY DAY

"Willingness to die is the price you must pay if you want to be raised from the dead to live and work and walk in the power of the third morning," Major Ian Thomas writes. "Once the willingness to die is there for us, there are no more issues to face, only instructions to obey."[11]

Walking in the power of the third morning. Practicing resurrection. More of Jesus and less of me. It all comes down to dying to self—of that, I am convinced. So was George Müller, the man I told you about earlier, whose work in England's orphanages made him famous in the last half of the nineteenth century:

> To one who asked him the secret of his service he said: "There was a day
> when I died, *utterly died*"; and, as he spoke, he bent lower and lower until he
> almost touched the floor—"died to George Müller, his opinions, preferences,
> tastes, and will—died to the world, its approval or censure—died to the
> approval or blame even of my brethren and friends—and since then I have
> studied only to show myself 'approved unto God.' "[12]

I don't know what that story does to you, but every time I read it, I feel compelled to hold yet another funeral in my own life...and then another. For while I wish I could tell you my resurrection required only one death and one burial, it wouldn't be true. Instead, my story has many obituaries.

Day by day, sometimes minute by minute, I must make that hard decision to deny myself so that I might obey God. Though Christ died once and for all, denying and dying is a daily exercise for those who would follow Him (1 Corinthians 15:31).

I can tell you this, however: Every day in which I've chosen to truly die, to lay down my wants and my wishes in order that Christ's wants and wishes might be realized in me, a little more of my sinful nature has died. And a little more resurrection has taken place.

However, there is another aspect of dying I'd like us to consider. A type of death we don't necessarily choose but is chosen for us. It involves a stripping away and purging of any excess in our lives. It's painful to endure and hard to understand at times. But it is necessary, because it makes room for Christ's life to grow in us.

Pruned by the Master's Hand

My mother is a master gardener. I wish you could sip iced tea with us as we look over her backyard. Every corner is filled with a beautiful tapestry of color that spills over her carefully edged flower beds. The scents are intoxicating and the fruits of her labor luscious as we eat raspberries just picked from the vine.

None of this beauty happened by accident. It has been carefully planned and tended with a lot of backbreaking work. As we walk through the garden, my mother points out each plant by name.

"This rosebush didn't bloom much last year, so I had to cut it back," she says, cradling a lovely blossom in her hand. "This peony had to be moved to get more sun, and I had to pull out a lot of irises to make room for more corn."

Her eyes glow warmly as she talks about her tasks, but what she describes is a series of seemingly brutal acts. Leafy branches chopped off. Healthy bushes pulled up by their roots. Blooming plants dug up and taken away. Each act is a certain kind of death. But all of it is done with love in the interest of summer bounty.

As I stroll with my mother through her garden, I'm reminded of the times I've questioned the One who tends the garden of my heart.

Especially during those times when His work felt more like death than life.

"I never knew suicide was so slow or so painful," I told my husband one night after falling into bed exhausted from an especially difficult period of battling my lower nature. But it wasn't just the "suicide" I was struggling with. It wasn't just my choosing to die to self. God seemed to be working me over as well.

It was the confusing period I wrote about in *Having a Mary Spirit* when God allowed a painful misunderstanding with friends to strip me of everything I had assumed I needed for life. Their love, their friendship, their kind understanding and support—all that was gone. And nothing I did made the situation better, only worse. The removal of their approval hurt me so deeply I thought I was going to die.

Which was the point, of course. But this wasn't the kind of death I had signed up for. I'd been expecting to close my eyes like Sleeping Beauty, then awaken refreshed and resurrected at the kiss of my handsome Savior Prince.

Instead, the Lord had showed up with sturdy gloves. I could almost see Him in blue jeans and a canvas hat, with a water bottle and a sack lunch protruding from a backpack. Was that a tent I saw? And in His hands—what were those?

A pair of heavy-duty shears.

For the "death" I was experiencing was really a season of pruning—lots and lots of pruning. It felt as though the Gardener was cutting off parts of me, pulling me up by the roots, taking away everything that gave testimony to life. The leafy branches that had once bloomed with color and dripped heavy with fruit had been stripped away, leaving me brown and bare and clinging to the trellis where I'd been tied.

Then came the long winter. And it too felt like death.

A SEASON OF DYING

Perhaps you are in a wintry season right now. Perhaps you feel as though everything you've cared about has been taken away, and you've not found anything to take its place. Perhaps God has called you to lay aside a lifetime of striving so you can experience abiding. But to be honest, the stillness is getting on your nerves. Perhaps He has narrowed you to a place where there is little choice but to be quiet. And listen. And wait.

Winter always seems to last longer than we think it should.

Getting through such times, I've learned, is not for the faint of heart. It's not easy to endure the loss of what we once thought was vital. To shiver in the dark, feeling bereft and confused. To wonder when—or if—this season of dying will ever end in true resurrection.

I understand how you feel. And so does Jesus—more than either of us knows. The One who hung forgotten and forsaken, cut down in the prime of His life and buried deep in the tomb, is so intimately acquainted with our suffering that He alone can remind us what is at stake.

"I tell you the truth," Jesus told His disciples after leaving the miracle of Bethany and beginning the hard walk toward Jerusalem and His death, "unless a kernel of wheat falls to the ground and dies, it remains only a single seed. But if it dies, it produces many seeds. The man who loves his life will lose it, while the man who hates his life in this world will keep it for eternal life" (John 12:24–25).

As strange as it sounds, it is in the dark nights of our souls—in those deathlike, midnight places where nothing seems to be happening—that God often does His best work. Preparing our lives—so barren at the moment—for an even greater outpouring of life.

For winter always precedes spring. And in the law of harvest, death always precedes life. But if we'll trust the Gardener, a harvest of fruit awaits—"much fruit," as John 15:5 calls it. Fruit formed out of the life of Christ released in us by our dying.

Abundant, luscious fruit that will last forever (verse 16).

It's amazing to think that so much life could come out of so much death. Yet that is the secret of living resurrected and the key to the exchanged life we need. Jesus alive in you and me. His power giving us all we need to do all He asks. His love, His joy, His peace and His righteousness being manifested in us. And none of it anything we have to do on our own.

Our only responsibility is to die. Jesus will take care of the rest. For He is not only the resurrection. He is also the life.

THE PROMISE OF NEW LIFE

After the women's conference in Lazarusville—not a real name, if you are wondering—I visited a vineyard just a few miles away. As a cold-climate girl from Montana, I was eager to get a closer look at how grapes are actually grown. It was early March, so the first place we stopped had no signs of life yet. Just ancient trunks protruding from the earth with woody vines trained upon thick wire. They were all brown and lifeless at that particular moment—just as I had felt from time to time during the preceding year.

However, as we drove deeper into the valley, we found another vineyard. This one was showing signs of life. Not much. Just a few touches of green among the brown.

"So how does it work?" I asked my hostess. "Is it like apple trees? Are there grape blossoms that have to be pollinated before the fruit can come?"

"I really don't know," my friend answered, perplexed, as she parked the car next to a row of grapevines.

I got out quickly, eager to look at the small clumps of leaves bursting out here and there along the vine. I had my camera and began to take pictures. But then I noticed something amazing.

Something profound.

There in the whorl of leaves slowly unfolding was a perfectly formed miniature cluster of grapes. Each and every tiny piece clearly defined. An exquisite embryo of promise. A not-yet picture of a one-day reality.

I can't begin to explain what I felt as the Holy Spirit later whispered to my heart, *See, Joanna? It's all there—all the potential, all the harvest that will one day be. The life of Christ was put within you at salvation, and He's just waiting to be fully revealed.*

All your striving isn't as necessary as your abiding, He seemed to say as I began to weep. *If you'll trust the seasons...if you're willing to die so that Jesus might live...it will happen. And the Gardener will get the glory.*

It's a word He may be speaking to you as well. Stop trying to produce fruit on your own, beloved. Let the Resurrection and the Life breathe color and beauty into your brown, barren being. Choose to die and embrace the intimate entangling of His life with yours. For there is a harvest within you that's been prepared in advance by God. A purpose for your life waiting to be revealed (Ephesians 2:10).

A Lazarus or a Lazarella in the making! A life meant to be fully lived, bursting with the fruit of righteousness. The type of life that has no explanation except this:

This person has died, and Christ now lives.

Soli Deo Gloria.

*Six days before the Passover, Jesus arrived
at Bethany, where Lazarus lived,
whom Jesus had raised from the dead.
Here a dinner was given in Jesus' honor.
Martha served, while Lazarus was among
those reclining at the table with him.
Then Mary took about a pint of pure nard, an expensive perfume;
she poured it on Jesus' feet and wiped his feet with her hair.
And the house was filled with the fragrance of the perfume.*

JOHN 12:1–3

Laughing Lazarus

During and after the Civil War, Sarah Winchester's husband acquired a fortune by manufacturing and selling the famous Winchester repeater rifles. But after his death in 1881, Sarah found herself tormented by grief over losing him and their infant daughter, who had died years before. Sarah sought out a medium to contact her dead husband. The medium said that her family was being haunted by the spirits of those killed by Winchester guns but that Sarah could appease those spirits if she moved out West and built a great house for them. "As long as you keep building it," the medium promised, "you will never face death."

Sarah believed the spiritualist, so she moved to San Jose, California, bought an unfinished eight-room house, and immediately started to expand it. Workers spent nearly four decades building and rebuilding the home—demolishing one section to build another, adding rooms onto rooms and wings onto wings. Staircases were built that led nowhere. Doors opened to nothing. Hallways doubled back throughout the house, creating a giant maze designed to confuse the spirits.

The project continued until Sarah died at the age of eighty-two. It cost more than five million dollars to build and featured 160 rooms, 13 bathrooms, 2,000 doors, 47 fireplaces, and 10,000 windows.

Today the Winchester house stands on a busy boulevard in San Jose, drawing thousands of visitors each year. But as one writer puts it, the house is "more than a tourist attraction. It is a silent witness to the dread of death."[1] The dread that has held humanity in bondage since the beginning of time.

The Fear of Death

For the majority of history, humanity has been plagued with a fear of dying—and with good reason. For the billions of people who lived before modern medicine, death was a daily reality, striking indiscriminately and often without obvious cause. One day a mother held her laughing child; the next day the child was dead from a mysterious fever. A husband would leave to hunt in the morning, only to be found gored to death by a wild animal in the afternoon. When a wife got pregnant, she faced heavy odds of dying in childbirth. Living to middle adulthood was considered quite an accomplishment.

I don't think those of us living in this century can fully appreciate the magnitude of hope Hebrews 2:14–15 must have brought those who read these words: "[Jesus] too shared in their humanity so that by his death he might destroy him who holds the power of death—that is, the devil—and *free those* who all their lives were *held in slavery by their fear of death*" (emphasis added).

While we're further removed from the constant reminders of our mortality, I think it's fair to say that none of us is looking forward to passing away. Woody Allen's famous quip describes our attitude: "I'm not afraid of dying—I just don't want to be there when it happens!"[2]

Perhaps that's why we spend billions of dollars each year attempting to halt or at least slow the march of time. We resolve to exercise, eat right, and take the proper multivitamins. We buy wonder foods and wonder drugs, scouring the Internet and magazines for the current fountain of youth.

Some people even go to the extreme of cryogenics, paying huge sums to have their bodies frozen just before they die in hopes that one day doctors will discover the secret to eternal life (or at least a cure for the disease about to kill them). A quick injection of serum, a few minutes in the microwave…and voilà! They'll be on the golf course the next day. Or so they hope.

But no matter how hard we try to outrun, outbuy, or outbuild death, in the end we will all breathe a last breath. For the cold, hard fact of life is this: we will all die.

That was true of Lazarus as well. Although Jesus dramatically raised him from the dead the first time, the man was *still* destined to die again. In fact, today you can visit two separate tombs that claim the distinction of having held Mary and

Martha's brother. The first one is in Bethany, now called al-Eizariya.[3] The second tomb is found on the island of Cyprus. According to Orthodox tradition, Lazarus served as bishop there for thirty years before passing away a final time.[4]

Although there's some controversy over where Lazarus was finally buried,[5] the fact remains: the one Jesus loved and gloriously resurrected eventually died a second time. Just as you and I will die one day. .

For there is no escaping death. But be assured of this: Death is not the end. There's more to come.

ENLISTING DEATH

God created us with a primal instinct for life and a violent resistance to death. There is a fight reflex within us that battles to breathe, scratching and clawing to the surface of whatever we're going through in order to survive. And that is as it should be. If we don't have a desire to live, then something is terribly wrong. Something has short-circuited our wiring, both physically and spiritually.

Because death was not part of God's original plan. You and I were made for life—life eternal. An eternity lived in the company of our Maker and each other.

Unfortunately, our great-great-not-so-great grandparents Adam and Eve decided they wanted more than what God had offered. So they bit at the serpent's bait and attempted to seize control as God's equals rather than resting in their role as His beloved children.

Consequently, the Father had to limit their freedom. He banished them from the garden and blocked access to the tree of life so they couldn't eat of it and "live forever" (Genesis 3:22). As a result, humanity's life span was radically reduced. Death was given access to beings who had been created to live forever.

Does that sound harsh? Although God's actions might seem extreme, we must understand that the punishment was birthed out of great mercy.

Just think. Without death, the evicted Adam and Eve—not to mention you and I—would be assigned to an eternity of lonely wandering. A 24/7 life of hopeless toil and meaningless monotony. An empty existence bereft of the constant sense of God's presence Adam and Eve had once enjoyed.

For two people who had once walked and talked with God, I can't imagine a more terrible destiny. Forever condemned to treading staircases leading nowhere. Running down hallways that circle back on themselves. Trying to find their way out of the confusing maze their rebellion had created.

What Will It Be Like?

In his commentary on the book of John, Ray Stedman retells a lovely story concerning death and what it will be like to cross from this life to the next.

> When Peter Marshall was Chaplain to the United States Senate, he told of a twelve-year-old boy who knew he was dying. The boy asked his father, "What is it like to die?" The father hugged his son to himself and said, "Son, do you remember when you were little and you used to come and sit on my lap in the big chair in the living room? I would tell you a story, read you a book, or sing you a song and you would go to sleep in my arms. Later, you would wake up in your own bed. That is what it's like to die. When you wake up from death, you are in a place of security and safety and beauty."

"That, Jesus declares, is what death is like," writes Stedman. "It is merely an introduction to another, greater experience of life. From our limited human perspective, we view death as a final farewell, a leap into mystery and darkness and silence. The death of a loved one leaves us feeling lonely and bereft, wandering alone through life. But Jesus says, 'No, death is [only] sleep.' "[6] There is more to come.

> *Brothers, we do not want you to be ignorant about those who fall*
> *asleep, or to grieve like the rest of men, who have no hope.*
> *We believe that Jesus died and rose again and so we believe*
> *that God will bring with Jesus those who have fallen asleep in him.*
> 1 Thessalonians 4:13–14

Which is a fairly accurate description of the life we live today when we attempt to live apart from God.

But here's the good news! God's mercy and grace marked our lives here on earth with a finish line. And with sweet irony, our loving Father took the very thing we feared the most—the threat of death—and turned it on its head. Transforming tombs into doorways and our endings into new beginnings. Turning hearses into glistening carriages to carry us to glorious mansions being prepared as we speak—the eternal home for which we were made (2 Corinthians 5:1).

And all of it ours if we will simply accept the gift Jesus offers—the gift of eternal life.

"Where, O death, is your victory?" Paul writes in 1 Corinthians 15:55 as he considers our final destination and the vehicle that will get us there. "Where, O death, is your sting?"

Through Jesus Christ, "death has been swallowed up in victory" (verse 54).

CROSSING OVER

Victory over death, however, isn't found only in the future. In a very real sense, for those who've received Christ, eternal life starts now. "If the Spirit of him that raised up Jesus from the dead dwell in you," Paul tells us in Romans 8:11 (KJV), "he...shall also *quicken* your mortal bodies by his Spirit that dwelleth in you" (emphasis added).

I love that old King James Version word *quicken*. It doesn't speak of speed but of coming to life. For you see, Jesus doesn't promise half a resurrection. He offers a full-fledged Holy Spirit CPR. A "get out the paddles because we're gonna quicken this guy" kind of life that crackles at the edges with passionate electricity!

Perhaps that's why Leonid Andreyev's portrait of a half-dead Lazarus doesn't ring true to me. The idea that Jesus would resurrect His friend to make him miserable is nothing like the Savior I know, nor is it anything like the mighty power of God I've experienced working in my life. When He resurrects, He resurrects completely.

Which is what happened to our spirits when we were saved. However, that's not to say there isn't more work to be done. Paul accentuates that point when he writes,

"But if Christ is in you, your body is dead because of sin, yet your spirit is alive because of righteousness" (Romans 8:10).

You see, it takes time—and some struggle—for our bodies and souls to catch up with what has happened in our spirits. Bringing resurrection into every part of life is both the joy and the struggle of our Christian walk. But we don't do it alone. It is a cooperative work with the Holy Spirit from beginning to end. The death in us is being conquered, and life is going to win!

So when I think of Lazarus, I don't picture a zombie walking around mad at the world, half-crazed. I don't picture him causing people to lose their minds when they looked in his eyes. Instead, I imagine him opening their minds to all the possibilities, all the sweet ramifications of a second chance at life.

After all, I can't think of anything more transformative, more freeing than facing the thing you fear most and finding it has no power. Talk about a new perspective!

LAZARUS LAUGHED

In my mind Lazarus resurrected would look more like the man depicted in Eugene O'Neill's play *Lazarus Laughed.* While you can't go to O'Neill for sound doctrine, the character he paints captures my heart and challenges my soul. The wonderful preacher John Claypool describes how the short-lived Broadway production depicted the resurrected Lazarus:

> O'Neill has Lazarus coming out of the tomb laughing. Not a bitter, scornful laughter, but a gentle, tender, all-pervasive kind of sound. After he is untied from the graveclothes, the first word he utters is, "YES!" He doesn't have a faraway look in his eyes, but rather, he seems to see the people closest to him with a new kind of delight and affection.... It is as if everything had taken on a new luster because of what he had learned. There was a kind of peace and serenity about him that was almost tangible....
>
> As the play unfolds, Lazarus embodies what it would mean to be freed of death. His house becomes called the house of laughter. There is music and

dancing there night and day, and as he continues to live in this free and wonderful way, other human beings are caught up in the joyfulness of it. They cease to be afraid. They start being generous and humane with one another. They fall back in love with the wonder of life itself.[7]

What would it be like if you and I could finally shed the fear of death and the grasping, clinging obsession with this world that comes with it? What if, in coming to terms with death, we were enabled to fall back in love with the wonder of life itself?

I'm fairly certain we'd experience more joy and less fear. More faith and less doubt. More love and less selfishness. More life in this life!

If we focused on living in the light of eternity, understanding that there is a glorious lifetime in a perfect world to come, I think we'd learn to hold this one more loosely and the ones we love less possessively. God wouldn't always have to do what you and I think is best. We'd see eternal possibilities in everyday troubles. We'd more easily surrender ourselves and those we love to God's plan rather than our demands.

Most of all I think we'd learn to live with an open hand rather than a clenched fist.

The Joy of Surrender

When I received word that my mother had suffered a massive heart attack and was being rushed into emergency surgery, I immediately began driving the 150 miles south to be with her. That was fourteen years ago, before I had a cell phone, so I had two hours without any updates, without any word of how the surgery was going. I wasn't even certain my mother was still alive.

But something amazing happened during my mad dash down the interstate. As I prayed and drove and prayed and drove some more, I found myself giving my mother to the Lord. Entrusting her to His care. Believing He would do what was best. And with the surrender came a sweet peace like none I'd ever known before. I knew it was going to be okay.

But please understand, I still didn't know if *she* would be okay. The peace I felt wasn't a promise that my mother would survive the surgery. In fact, I found out later that she actually died on the table for a few minutes. The peace that enfolded me as I drove toward the unknown promised only this:

It would be okay. Whatever *it* turned out to be.

As I opened my hand and surrendered my mom to the God who loved her even more than I did, I felt a quiet joy fill my heart. A sweet underlying sense of okayness that surpassed happiness (which tends to rely heavily on happenings).

The settled peace I felt was a gift from the Lord, not something I could have worked up on my own. Lazarus must have felt that same peace when he walked out of the tomb and back into life—but magnified a hundredfold and tinged with amazing joy.

For he had traveled to the place we humans avoid at all cost and had found God waiting there.

When Tombs Don't Open

Like Mary and Martha, I was blessed to receive my loved one—my mother—back from the brink of death. Yet I'm painfully aware that you may be among the many who've stood before tombs that haven't opened.

You've prayed desperate prayers that were left unanswered. Perhaps, like Job, you've struggled to reconcile your faith in a loving God with a seemingly less-than-loving outcome. You've lain in bed at night wondering how to keep believing that God is good when everything in your life feels so terribly bad.

Over the past twelve months especially, I've had a glimpse of how that must feel. It's been such a strange year for me. In the midst of writing about the miracle-working power of God to rescue and resurrect, I've attended more funerals and witnessed more tragedies than in the past six years combined. Among my friends there have been two massive heart attacks, one severe stroke, three premature deaths due to cancer, the tragic death of a son, and the suicide of a distraught father—to name a few. In June my own dad had a serious subdural hematoma in his brain and then was diagnosed with renal cancer five months later. Three weeks after that my husband was operated on twice for kidney stones.

Through it all, we've run the gamut of emotions: dancing gratefully in hospital waiting rooms one moment, weeping beside snow-covered graves the next.

And through it all, like you, we've hung onto Jesus when the whys of it all were totally beyond us.

I can't begin to fully explain God's ways or why He allows pain and suffering to coexist beside His intense love for us. But I do wonder if He doesn't want to use all the sorrow I've recently witnessed to balance the message He would have me write in this book.

It is far too easy to preach a Pollyanna gospel—a gospel that says if we're good, nothing bad should ever happen. A formula Christianity that is neat and tidy, suggesting that if we play by the rules, we'll win every time.

The story of Lazarus refutes all that. As does the whole of the Bible. Scripture never shies away from the reality that bad things happen to good people. That God doesn't always come running to the rescue, at least not in the ways and in the timing we expect Him to. Love does tarry at times. And there are moments when Love seems to actually take a step back, allowing things to happen that we'd never dream of allowing ourselves.

Just ask Joseph as he scratches yet another day on the wall of his prison cell, counting the long years since he dreamed God's dream and wondering how and when he lost God's favor.

Just ask Daniel as he wraps his cloak around his shoulders and shivers in the pit, half from the cold and half from fear of the lions breathing hot upon his neck—all because Daniel wouldn't deny his God.

And just ask John, the disciple who told us the most about Lazarus. Years later he's an old man exiled and left to starve on the barren island of Patmos. One by one he's heard about the demise of his friends—martyrdom after brutal martyrdom for the men who had followed Christ. The disciples had proven faithful, following Jesus all the way to their deaths. Would he be next?

In each seemingly hopeless case, however, Love's restraint eventually accomplished God's purposes. Saving Egypt and the known world—not to mention Joseph's brothers!—from starvation in a famine. Exalting God among a pagan nation as the one true God, who is able to shut lions' mouths and turn the hearts of kings. And providing us a glimpse of eternity (the book of Revelation) through the pen of a lonely old man.

The same tender-yet-tough-to-understand divine restraint may be required in your life and mine. But it will also accomplish God's purposes if we'll trust Him. Though we may never know the full story here on earth, we can be certain that nothing in our lives will be wasted by God. Trials and tragedies, even death, can't separate us from His love (Romans 8:39). Especially when we surrender our questions and our need to understand, entrusting all our confusion and fear to His heart and to His hands.

GETTING READY FOR THE REAL THING

I'm starting to wonder if one reason God allows difficulties in our lives is to wean us from this world, to cure our addiction to temporal things that will never satisfy. Because it seems that the times we come face to face with pain and death are the times we're reminded best that this world is just a shadow. A crude drawing and a mere outline of the beauty that awaits us in a world outside this one. An alternate reality so magnificent and incomprehensible that we often forget it's there.

In his marvelous book *Things Unseen,* Mark Buchanan tells the story of a couple who lost their barely born son due to a rare and severe genetic disorder. Three months later their two-year-old daughter died as well. In the wake of devastating loss, Marshall and Susan Shelley wrestled painfully with God. *Why, God?* they kept asking. *Why did You do that? What was all that about?*[8]

Marshall later shared his struggle to understand his son's death in an article he wrote for *Christianity Today.* "Why did God create a child to live two minutes?" he asked before answering:

> He didn't. [And] He didn't create Mandy to live two years. He did not create me to live 40 years (or whatever number he may choose to extend my days in this world).
>
> God created Toby for eternity. He created each of us for eternity, where we may be surprised to find our true calling, which always seemed just out of reach here on earth.[9]

What a powerful thought! We were not created for this earth alone but for an infinite future with God. A destiny beyond the realm of mere time and space. How would our lives change if we really woke up to that reality?

Is it just me, or have we lost this sense of another world awaiting us as Christians? Have we become so attached to this world and its comforts that we've forgotten we are only pilgrims? Aliens as it were—created for another place. This life just a spaceship meant to carry us through this world to our one true home.

I love the way Elisabeth Elliot describes it:

> Heaven is not *here,* it's *There.* If we were given all we wanted here, our hearts would settle for this world rather than the next. God is forever luring us up and away from this one, wooing us to Himself and His still invisible Kingdom, where we will certainly find what we so keenly long for.[10]

LONELY FOR HOME

Someone once asked, "Why do we tend to live like eternity lasts eighty years, but this life lasts forever?"

It's an important question, I think. As a young Christian, I realized that if I were to draw a time line of eternity, then attempted to place my lifetime on that continuum, it wouldn't even show up. In reality, these eighty-plus years we're given are only a blip on the screen, a "vapor," as James 4:14 (NKJV) describes it. A mist that quickly fades away.

Some people, even some Christians, don't believe there is anything after this life. From their perspective, we live and then we die. Dust to dust, ashes to ashes. Worm food. They say there's no such thing as resurrection and Jesus isn't coming back. Heaven, if there is a heaven, is found right here on earth.

And in a sense they are partly right. Heaven began on earth when, through Christ, the "kingdom of heaven" came near (Matthew 4:17). For those who have put their full hope in Jesus, eternity has already begun.

But to say this is all there is? I can't think of anything more disappointing or sad. For if the limited taste of heaven we experience here on earth is all we have to look forward to, then why bother?

Living in the Light of Eternity

In light of the fact that there is more to come, how then shall we live? If eternity, not this earth, is our true home, don't you think we should live differently than the world does? I'd like to suggest these principles:

- *Live fully.* Don't waste today regretting the past or fearing the future, for it may be your last day on earth. Make it count for God.
- *Hold things loosely.* Since we can't take our possessions with us, enjoy what you have, but don't cling so tightly to stuff or fall into the trap of always wanting more.
- *Value people highly.* People are the true treasures of life, worth nurturing and investing in, for they are the only thing on this earth we can possibly take with us when we leave.
- *Travel lightly.* Don't carry baggage from past hurts, and don't pick up grudges as you go. Life's too short to be voluntarily miserable.
- *Love completely.* Let God reveal His love for people through you. Be tender-hearted, not hardheaded, patient and quick to forgive, merciful and slow to judge.
- *Give freely.* Don't hoard what you have. Instead, share it with a joyful heart, and you'll be given more. Generosity releases blessings as sowing seed leads to harvest.
- *Look expectantly.* Keep looking up even as you walk here on earth, always ready and waiting for the imminent return of Christ. Be heavenly minded so you can be of earthly good.

So then, dear friends, since you are looking forward
to [Christ's return], make every effort
to be found spotless, blameless and at peace with him.

2 PETER 3:14

The apostle Paul agreed. "If there is no resurrection of the dead, then not even Christ has been raised," he argues in 1 Corinthians 15:13–14. "And if Christ has not been raised, our preaching is useless and so is your faith."

Paul was fully convinced that eternity is what matters—not this puny little life we tend so carefully. In fact, Paul makes an incredibly bold statement that should shake not only the way we think but impact the way we live. "If only for this life we have hope in Christ, we are to be pitied more than all men" (1 Corinthians 15:19).

In other words, if this is all there is, folks, we're in big trouble.

That's why living in the light of eternity is so very important. If we don't cultivate an eternal perspective, we will get bogged down in both the blessings and the troubles of this life. We'll tend to become obsessed about success, possessed by our possessions, and addicted to our appetite for more, more, always more.

We may call Jesus our friend. We may even declare Him our most prized possession, saying that He is more than enough. But if we fail to think eternally, chances are we'll tend to hold tightly to everything we can fit in our overcrowded arms for fear that this is all there is and we had better get what we can get while the getting is good.

But this isn't the life we were made for. In fact, it is not life at all. It's just another tomb. Better wallpapered, perhaps, with finer furnishings. But still just a tomb.

The Last Laugh

Lazarus knew that this earthly life isn't what we were made for. And I think he must have laughed. Because in the experience of dying and being resurrected, Lazarus must have discovered there was so much more to living than what he had known. To his reborn eyes, the life he'd been attached to, the one that had seemed so fraught with difficulty, must have looked like child's play.

From his brief glimpse of eternity, Lazarus could surely discern the counterfeit from the genuine. The cardboard facsimiles we work so hard to build. The papier-mâché dreams that occupy our hearts and minds. The silly games we play. The inconsequential things we inflate until they seem monumental.

The resurrected Lazarus surely saw life differently because he knew there was more to come. If we could only grasp that, Lazarus wouldn't be the only one laughing.

For a day is coming that will cause joy like we've never known to well up within us. A laughter that will be triggered by a trumpet and echoed by a magnificent figure on a great white horse, waving the keys of hell, death, and the grave over his head as He comes riding toward us in triumph (Revelation 1:18).

Christ Himself. Our Savior. Once entombed, now alive. Risen and gone to be with the Father. But returning again. We can be sure of that!

> For the Lord himself will come down from heaven, with a loud command,
> with the voice of the archangel and with the trumpet call of God, and the
> dead in Christ will rise first. After that, we who are still alive and are left will
> be caught up together with them in the clouds to meet the Lord in the air.
> And so we will be with the Lord forever. Therefore encourage each other with
> these words. (1 Thessalonians 4:16–18)

What an amazing day that is going to be! We don't know *when* it will happen, but we can be sure it *will* happen. It's written in black and white all over the Word. But more important, it's been signed and sealed in red—by the precious blood of Jesus Christ.

"Do not let your hearts be troubled," Jesus told the disciples shortly after He had raised Lazarus. "Trust in God; trust also in me. In my Father's house are many rooms.... I am going there to prepare a place for you. And if I go and prepare a place for you, I will come back and take you to be with me that you also may be where I am" (John 14:1–3).

Jesus is coming back. He's coming back for me and you. And what He has prepared for us will rival anything Sarah Winchester could have ever imagined. More rooms, more doors, so many more windows! He's building a mansion—"many mansions," the King James Version of John 14:2 tells us—and all of it for His Bride.

For it is love that compels Him. Love for you and me and everyone else who has ever responded to the sound of His voice. Pulling at our graveclothes as we stumble out of our tombs. Running smack-dab into the tender arms of our Lord. Laughing and crying at the same time as we join Him for the ultimate celebration that is to come.

YOUR PLACE AT THE TABLE

I wish I could have been there at the dinner Mary and Martha threw for Jesus, the man who had brought their brother back to life. John 12:1–3 describes it like this:

> Six days before the Passover, Jesus arrived at Bethany, where Lazarus lived, whom Jesus had raised from the dead. Here a dinner was given in Jesus' honor. Martha served, while Lazarus was among those reclining at the table with him. Then Mary took about a pint of pure nard, an expensive perfume; she poured it on Jesus' feet and wiped his feet with her hair. And the house was filled with the fragrance of the perfume.

What a tender picture of sweet communion. I can picture Martha bringing in her platters of succulent food but this time lingering to listen while her Master spoke. I can see Mary hanging on His every word but also being stirred in her heart to anoint the Lord with the very best she had to give. I can't help but wonder if John, the beloved disciple, didn't give up his regular seat so that Lazarus could have a chance to lean against Jesus. The beautiful fragrance that filled the house surely came from more than Mary's perfume.

But as lovely as the scene must have been, it was also tense. Death threats against Jesus—and against Lazarus—were circulating in the village. Although many people were putting their faith in the Lord because of the miracle, others feared Jesus's growing influence. Even a few of His followers were uncomfortable with the way things were going.

When Mary poured an entire jar of precious perfume over Jesus's feet, Judas Iscariot may not have been the only one who thought it was a waste. But Jesus commended Mary's extravagant offering. "Leave her alone," He said. "It was intended that she should save this perfume for the day of my burial" (verse 7).

You see, the Lord knew His time on earth was coming to a close. It would be the last meal He shared in Bethany with His dear friends. Tender memories must have filled Jesus's mind as He watched Martha serve and Lazarus recline. When Mary bent to spread the perfume with her hair, her love must have washed over His heart as well as His feet.

The description of this meal is especially significant to me, because it is the last time we find the family from Bethany mentioned in Scripture. After spending more than a decade imagining and writing about their lives, I long to meet Mary and Martha and Lazarus in person.

And someday I will! For when the trumpet sounds, we will all meet Jesus in the air. Then later, in heaven, the family from Bethany and the rest of the family of God will sit down together at a sumptuous feast—the marriage supper of the Lamb (Revelation 19:9).

With that thought in mind, may I ask you a few personal questions?

When you think of that glorious day, where do you see yourself sitting? What do you see yourself doing? Will you kneel adoringly at Jesus's feet…or sit close to talk to Him as you hand Him a plate of food? Will you run to Him like a child and climb up on His lap…or look deep in His eyes before falling to your knees in worship? Just imagine how wonderful that is going to be.

Then let me ask you, are you doing that here?

Are you drawing as close to Jesus as you can possibly get while you live for Him here on earth? Shedding your love-doubt and your fear of the yardstick so you can run to Him daily as a friend runs to meet a friend?

First Corinthians 13:12 (KJV) seems to suggest that we will be known in heaven as we are known on earth. And that, I believe, should have radical implications for how we live our lives each day. I don't want to wait until I get to heaven to know Jesus. I want to snuggle up close to Him today.

I want to lay my head on His chest and hear His heart beat as the disciple John did (John 21:20, KJV).

I want to lay my greatest treasures down at His feet as Mary did.

I want to serve the Lord wholeheartedly yet respond to His rebuke and change as Martha did.

Most of all I want to laugh like Lazarus—laugh aloud with pure wonder that I belong to Jesus and He belongs to me. That nothing, absolutely nothing, will ever separate me from His love. Not the trials of this life nor the trinkets of this world. For I am my Beloved's, and He is mine (Song of Songs 6:3).

In 890 AD, when the supposed tomb of Mary and Martha's brother was discovered on Cyprus, the marble sarcophagus they found was marked with a simple inscription: "Lazarus...friend of Christ."[11]

I can't think of a better way to be defined—in life or in death. Both *here* on earth as well as *there* someday. For this world is not our home. We're just passing through.

So let's keep living as if we're dying, keeping eternity ever in view. Especially when life is hard and we don't understand. When love seems to tarry and we're tempted to doubt God's love and give up hope.

For it's in times like these, my friend, that we must remember...

There's more to come.

The Story

John 11:1–12:11

JOHN 11

[1] Now a man named Lazarus was sick. He was from Bethany, the village of Mary and her sister Martha. [2] This Mary, whose brother Lazarus now lay sick, was the same one who poured perfume on the Lord and wiped his feet with her hair. [3] So the sisters sent word to Jesus, "Lord, the one you love is sick."

[4] When he heard this, Jesus said, "This sickness will not end in death. No, it is for God's glory so that God's Son may be glorified through it." [5] Jesus loved Martha and her sister and Lazarus. [6] Yet when he heard that Lazarus was sick, he stayed where he was two more days.

[7] Then he said to his disciples, "Let us go back to Judea."

[8] "But Rabbi," they said, "a short while ago the Jews tried to stone you, and yet you are going back there?"

[9] Jesus answered, "Are there not twelve hours of daylight? A man who walks by day will not stumble, for he sees by this world's light. [10] It is when he walks by night that he stumbles, for he has no light."

[11] After he had said this, he went on to tell them, "Our friend Lazarus has fallen asleep; but I am going there to wake him up."

[12] His disciples replied, "Lord, if he sleeps, he will get better." [13] Jesus had been speaking of his death, but his disciples thought he meant natural sleep.

[14] So then he told them plainly, "Lazarus is dead, [15] and for your sake I am glad I was not there, so that you may believe. But let us go to him."

[16] Then Thomas (called Didymus) said to the rest of the disciples, "Let us also go, that we may die with him."

[17] On his arrival, Jesus found that Lazarus had already been in the tomb for four days. [18] Bethany was less than two miles from Jerusalem, [19] and many Jews had come to Martha and Mary to comfort them in the loss of their brother. [20] When Martha heard that Jesus was coming, she went out to meet him, but Mary stayed at home.

[21] "Lord," Martha said to Jesus, "if you had been here, my brother would not have died. [22] But I know that even now God will give you whatever you ask."

[23] Jesus said to her, "Your brother will rise again."

[24] Martha answered, "I know he will rise again in the resurrection at the last day."

[25] Jesus said to her, "I am the resurrection and the life. He who believes in me will live, even though he dies; [26] and whoever lives and believes in me will never die. Do you believe this?"

[27] "Yes, Lord," she told him, "I believe that you are the Christ, the Son of God, who was to come into the world."

[28] And after she had said this, she went back and called her sister Mary aside. "The Teacher is here," she said, "and is asking for you." [29] When Mary heard this, she got up quickly and went to him. [30] Now Jesus had not yet entered the village, but was still at the place where Martha had met him. [31] When the Jews who had been with Mary in the house, comforting her, noticed how quickly she got up and went out, they followed her, supposing she was going to the tomb to mourn there.

[32] When Mary reached the place where Jesus was and saw him, she fell at his feet and said, "Lord, if you had been here, my brother would not have died."

[33] When Jesus saw her weeping, and the Jews who had come along with her also weeping, he was deeply moved in spirit and troubled. [34] "Where have you laid him?" he asked.

"Come and see, Lord," they replied.

[35] Jesus wept.

[36] Then the Jews said, "See how he loved him!"

[37] But some of them said, "Could not he who opened the eyes of the blind man have kept this man from dying?"

³⁸ Jesus, once more deeply moved, came to the tomb. It was a cave with a stone laid across the entrance. ³⁹ "Take away the stone," he said.

"But, Lord," said Martha, the sister of the dead man, "by this time there is a bad odor, for he has been there four days."

⁴⁰ Then Jesus said, "Did I not tell you that if you believed, you would see the glory of God?"

⁴¹ So they took away the stone. Then Jesus looked up and said, "Father, I thank you that you have heard me. ⁴² I knew that you always hear me, but I said this for the benefit of the people standing here, that they may believe that you sent me."

⁴³ When he had said this, Jesus called in a loud voice, "Lazarus, come out!" ⁴⁴ The dead man came out, his hands and feet wrapped with strips of linen, and a cloth around his face.

Jesus said to them, "Take off the grave clothes and let him go."

⁴⁵ Therefore many of the Jews who had come to visit Mary, and had seen what Jesus did, put their faith in him. ⁴⁶ But some of them went to the Pharisees and told them what Jesus had done. ⁴⁷ Then the chief priests and the Pharisees called a meeting of the Sanhedrin.

"What are we accomplishing?" they asked. "Here is this man performing many miraculous signs. ⁴⁸ If we let him go on like this, everyone will believe in him, and then the Romans will come and take away both our place and our nation."

⁴⁹ Then one of them, named Caiaphas, who was high priest that year, spoke up, "You know nothing at all! ⁵⁰ You do not realize that it is better for you that one man die for the people than that the whole nation perish."

⁵¹ He did not say this on his own, but as high priest that year he prophesied that Jesus would die for the Jewish nation, ⁵² and not only for that nation but also for the scattered children of God, to bring them together and make them one. ⁵³ So from that day on they plotted to take his life.

⁵⁴ Therefore Jesus no longer moved about publicly among the Jews. Instead he withdrew to a region near the desert, to a village called Ephraim, where he stayed with his disciples.

⁵⁵ When it was almost time for the Jewish Passover, many went up from the country to Jerusalem for their ceremonial cleansing before the Passover. ⁵⁶ They kept

looking for Jesus, and as they stood in the temple area they asked one another, "What do you think? Isn't he coming to the Feast at all?" [57] But the chief priests and Pharisees had given orders that if anyone found out where Jesus was, he should report it so that they might arrest him.

JOHN 12

[1] Six days before the Passover, Jesus arrived at Bethany, where Lazarus lived, whom Jesus had raised from the dead. [2] Here a dinner was given in Jesus' honor. Martha served, while Lazarus was among those reclining at the table with him. [3] Then Mary took about a pint of pure nard, an expensive perfume; she poured it on Jesus' feet and wiped his feet with her hair. And the house was filled with the fragrance of the perfume.

[4] But one of his disciples, Judas Iscariot, who was later to betray him, objected, [5] "Why wasn't this perfume sold and the money given to the poor? It was worth a year's wages." [6] He did not say this because he cared about the poor but because he was a thief; as keeper of the money bag, he used to help himself to what was put into it.

[7] "Leave her alone," Jesus replied. "It was intended that she should save this perfume for the day of my burial. [8] You will always have the poor among you, but you will not always have me."

[9] Meanwhile a large crowd of Jews found out that Jesus was there and came, not only because of him but also to see Lazarus, whom he had raised from the dead. [10] So the chief priests made plans to kill Lazarus as well, [11] for on account of him many of the Jews were going over to Jesus and putting their faith in him.

Study Guide

With just a word Jesus called Lazarus from the grave, and His Word can help bring us out of our tombs as well. This ten-week Bible study is designed to help you move toward your own Lazarus awakening. (Group leaders, if an eight-week format works better for you, you'll find directions at the end of this guide for adapting it. Also, check out the downloadable workbook and leader's guide available at www.joannaweaverbooks.com.)

Any translation of the Bible you enjoy and understand will work fine for this study (though I have used the NIV to word my questions). You'll also need a notebook and a pen to record your answers to the questions in this guide. Before each lesson ask the Holy Spirit to increase your understanding as you examine God's Word so that you can apply the truths you discover.

Each lesson starts with questions for individual reflection or group discussion, then moves into a "Going Deeper" study of scriptural principles. At the end of the lesson, you'll have an opportunity to write about or discuss what spoke most to you in that chapter. The stories, quotes, and sidebars within the chapters may provide further opportunities for discussion or reflection.

"I will walk about in freedom, for I have sought out your precepts," Psalm 119:45 tells us. The same freedom awaits each one of us as we set our hearts on knowing God's Word. Prayerfully commit yourself to this study, giving God access to every tomb that keeps you from living resurrected. For Love is calling your name.

Are you ready to "come forth"?

CHAPTER ONE: TALE
OF THE THIRD FOLLOWER

Questions for Discussion or Reflection

1. This chapter mentions my difficulty with algebra in high school. What was your best subject in school? What was your worst?

2. Look at the sidebar titled "What Kind of Father Do You Have?" on page 4. Which (if any) misrepresentation of God as Father have you struggled with? Have you experienced another kind not named? How do you think your connection with your earthly father has affected your relationship with God?

Going Deeper

3. Consider the words of David in Psalm 22:1, echoed by Jesus on the cross. Scripture is filled with people who struggled with love-doubt. What kind of circumstances in your life have caused you to question God's love? What has helped you get God's love from your head to your heart?

4. Read the story of Lazarus found in John 11:1–12:11 (or see Appendix A). Circle or underline key phrases. What stands out to you most in this passage, and why?

5. Put yourself in the sandals of Mary, Martha, or Lazarus. Write a letter to Jesus from that person's perspective. You can choose any point on the time line of the story.

6. What do the following verses reveal about the love God has for us?
   Psalm 86:15 _____
   Romans 8:35–39 _____
   1 John 3:1 _____

7. Write out Ephesians 3:17–19 on an index card, beginning with the words "I pray." Refer to the card frequently over the next few days, memorizing the passage phrase by phrase. Repeat it until it becomes a part of you.

8. What spoke most to you in this chapter?

Chapter Two: Lord, the One You Love Is Sick

Questions for Discussion or Reflection

1. Describe briefly how you came to know Jesus as your personal Savior. (If you haven't yet received the gift He offers, why not do it today? Look at "The Invitation" on page 27.)

2. If you were to send a message to Jesus concerning your current situation and need, how would you fill in the blank: "Lord, the one you love is _____"?

Going Deeper

3. Sin is deadly and separates us from God. Match the downward spiral of sin and its effects listed below to the following scriptures by filling in the appropriate letter in the blank before the phrase: (a) Psalm 106:43; (b) Acts 8:23; (c) James 1:14–15.

____ Fills us with bitterness   ____ Enticed by our own evil desires

____ Makes us waste away   ____ Holds us captive

____ Ends in death   ____ Causes us to rebel against God

4. Read "What God Does with Our Sins" (pages 24–25). Which one of the points listed by Rosalind Goforth speaks most to your heart? Look up the accompanying scripture and then write it out in your own words.

5. How does Satan—not to mention your own lower nature—tend to lull you to sleep spiritually, even though you're a Christian?

6. Consider the following verses. According to these scriptures, why is it so important that we wake up, and what should our awakening involve?

Matthew 25:1–13 _____

Romans 13:11–12 _____

Ephesians 5:11–15 _____

7. "God is not mad at you!" That's the best part of the gospel, someone has said. In fact, instead of holding a grudge, the Lord wants to forgive us and make us His own. Look up the following scriptures and really meditate on them. Under each reference listed below, write down keywords or phrases that reveal God's attitude toward us.

Isaiah 44:21–22   2 Corinthians 5:17–21   Colossians 1:21–23a

8. What spoke most to you in this chapter?

CHAPTER THREE: OUR FRIEND LAZARUS

Questions for Discussion or Reflection

1. Describe a moment—big or small—when you felt especially loved. What were the circumstances, and what people were involved? Why do you think that experience was so special to you?

2. Take the test found in the sidebar titled "What Kind of Friend Am I?" on pages 44–45. What did you discover about your relationship with God? with others? Share one aspect of friendship in which you'd like to grow.

Going Deeper

3. How do you respond to the idea that God is an emotional God, feeling deep loneliness and a need for connection? Do you find that possibility

comforting or frightening? Read Genesis 2:18–3:13. What do you think God felt when Adam and Eve chose to disobey? If He had penned a journal entry that day long ago, what might it have said?

4. Read Hebrews 8:10–12, which describes the new covenant God has made with you and me. If we really understood and responded to His deep desire for fellowship, how would our perspective change toward the following things we do as Christians?

     Daily prayer and reading the Bible: _____
     Attending church: _____
     Living a holy life: _____

5. The statements below describe three famous friends of God: Abraham, Moses, and David. Using Numbers 12:7–8, Acts 13:22, and James 2:21–23 as references, match each characteristic below with one of these friends. Do any of these qualities apply to you, even in a small way?

     _____ He was a man after God's own heart.
     _____ He was faithful in all God's house.
     _____ His faith and actions worked together.
     _____ He would do everything God wanted him to do.
     _____ He believed God, and it was credited to him as righteousness.
     _____ God spoke clearly to him and not in riddles.

6. Read John 15:13–17. Write down what you discover in this passage about being a friend of Jesus.

7. Read "Help Me Love You More!" on page 38. How would you fill in the blank in the sidebar? Write your own prayer to the Lord, asking Him to increase your ability to love Him better and more.

8. What spoke most to you in this chapter?

Chapter Four: When Love Tarries

Questions for Discussion or Reflection

1. Describe a time in your life when waiting was especially difficult. How did you react to the process, and what did you learn?

2. Delayed gratification is difficult for all of us. Consider the following aspects, and identify which one (or ones) you struggled with most while growing up and which is hardest for you today. If possible, give specific examples.
   - Adapting to less-than-perfect situations
   - Waiting for the fulfillment of our needs or desires
   - Accepting not only delays but also denials of what we want
   - Other: _____

Going Deeper

3. One of the hardest things for many people to understand about God is that He doesn't always interrupt or intervene when we're in trouble. Instead, He specializes in redeeming the situation, using it for our good and His kingdom. Look at the following passages and write down the problem God allowed and the benefit that eventually resulted.

   Acts 7:59–8:3   *Problem:* _____
   Acts 11:19–21   *Result:* _____

   Acts 21:30–36   *Problem:* _____
   Philippians 1:12–14 *Result:* _____

4. We humans tend to love formulas—if we do A and we do B, then God will have to do C. Read Isaiah 55:8–9 and Romans 11:33–36 several times, and allow the heavenly perspective to sink into your heart. Write a response to the Lord concerning the ways you may have tried to control Him through "formulas" rather than simply trusting He knows what is best.

5. Read "The Blessing of Trouble" sidebar on pages 58–59. Think of a time when you asked God for something and *didn't* get what you asked for. How has that experience affected your character and your life? Do you think you grew from the experience? Why or why not?

6. What do the following verses have to say about the benefits of waiting? Circle the benefit that means the most to you.

     Psalm 40:1–3 _____

     Isaiah 64:4 _____

     Lamentations 3:24–27 _____

7. In what area of your life do you need to hand God the "quill of your will"? Read Romans 8:28 and write it back to the Lord as a prayer, replacing "all things" with specific details of your situation. End the prayer with a declaration of your love and commitment to His will.

8. What spoke most to you in this chapter?

CHAPTER FIVE: TOMB DWELLING

Questions for Discussion or Reflection

1. An old New Mexico tombstone reads, "Here lies Johnny Yeast. Pardon me for not rising."[1] Another one in Colorado protests, "I told you I was sick!" These are silly epitaphs, but on a more serious note, what would you like your grave marker to say?

2. Consider the "Hurts, Hang-ups, and Habits" sidebar on page 70. Which of these three categories of strongholds tends to trip you up most often in your walk with God? If you feel comfortable sharing, name at least one item you're struggling with (or have given in to!) right now. Privately or as a group, take those things to the Lord in prayer, claiming the promise of James 5:16.

Going Deeper

3. The Bible speaks powerfully to so many issues. Using a concordance, look up a word or assorted words that relate to your particular struggle—lust, anger, pride, fear, lying, whatever you may be facing. (If needed, ask a friend experienced in Bible study to help.) Pick three pertinent verses to write down, then choose one to memorize.

4. We all have lies in our lives that have been internalized as truth. In order to uncover false beliefs, consider the following questions. (Don't discount anything, even seemingly small stuff that has happened or innocent pastimes you tend to turn to for escape.)

   • What failure or trauma from your past still defines you as though it's your *identity*?
   • What coping mechanism do you regularly turn to for *security*?
   • In the words of self-help guru Dr. Phil, "How's that workin' for ya?"

5. According to the following verses, why is it so important for us to acknowledge our need of forgiveness and healing?

    Psalm 66:18–20 _____

    Isaiah 30:15–16 _____

    1 John 1:9–10 _____

6. The book of Isaiah gives us many glimpses into the purpose of Jesus's coming and ministry. Under the corresponding verses, list the things you discover.

    Isaiah 42:1–4   Isaiah 61:1–3

7. One of the most precious aspects of God's work in our lives is His ability to redefine us and change our identities. For the following verses, write down the old name and the new name given and the significance of each. Then consider Revelation 2:17 and its significance to you.

   Genesis 32:24–28   Old name: _____

                        New name: _____

                        Significance: _____

   Matthew 16:13–18   Old name: _____

                        New name: _____

                        Significance: _____

   Revelation 2:17   Significance: _____

8. What spoke most to you in this chapter?

CHAPTER SIX: ROLL AWAY THE STONE

Questions for Discussion or Reflection

1. Rolling away stones can be hard. Physically speaking, what is the hardest thing you've ever done (climbed a mountain, given birth, etc.)? Describe the experience.

2. Without giving unnecessary details, share a time when bringing a secret to light destroyed the power it had exerted over you.

Going Deeper

3. Craig Groeschel says that many of us are *Christian atheists*—"believing in God but living as if He doesn't exist." Can you see signs of this contradiction in your life or in the lives of Christians in general? Give an example (big or little) if you can. What could we do to better fight the tendency toward Christian atheism?

4. Read through Psalm 91 and consider the benefits of making God our shelter and dwelling place rather than choosing to remain in our tombs. List five benefits you appreciate, then pick the one that means the most to you, and write a short paragraph explaining why.

5. God went out of His way to remove the barrier that stood between us and Him. Look up the following passages and fill in the blanks.

   Leviticus 16:2   The barrier: _____

   Matthew 27:50–51   The process: _____

   Hebrews 10:19–22   The result: _____

6. Which one of the following "stones" might be blocking God's access to the places in you that need healing? Look up the corresponding verses, and paraphrase your favorite part back to the Lord as a prayer, asking for help to remove it so that you might be free. Can you think of any other stones—besides these three—that might be keeping you from Him?
   - *Unworthiness* (Romans 4:7–8; 8:1)
   - *Unforgiveness* (Ephesians 4:31–5:2)
   - *Unbelief* (Romans 4:20–22)

7. As you hear Jesus asking you to roll away the boulder blockading your heart, what does His response to Martha mean to you: "Did I not tell you that if you believed, you would see the glory of God?" (John 11:40)? What would it take for you to lay aside unbelief and move forward in your process of healing?

8. What spoke most to you in this chapter?

Chapter Seven: When Love Calls Your Name

Questions for Discussion or Reflection

1. Did you have a nickname growing up? What did your mom call you when you were in trouble?

2. If you were administered a spiritual hearing test today, what do you think the results would be? (Check one.)

____ Excellent

____ Improving

____ Average

____ Poor

____ Acute deafness

Is hearing from God a personal struggle for you? What do you normally do to improve your hearing?

Going Deeper

3. Read the passage from Priscilla Shirer on page 105. In what ways, past or present, has the Enemy tried to convince you that you can't or don't hear God's voice?

4. Elijah heard from God in 1 Kings 19:11–12, but not in the way he expected. What does this passage of Scripture and Isaiah 30:21 reveal about how God tends to speak to us today? What makes the first part of Psalm 46:10 so important to improving our ability to hear Him?

5. Matthew 7:24–27 highlights the importance of obeying when God speaks and warns what happens when we don't. Record the two different responses to the Lord's words you find in the following verses and the outcome of each.

Matthew 7:24–25   *Response:* _____

Result: _____

Matthew 7:26–27   *Response:* _____

Result: _____

6. If possible, describe a time when the Holy Spirit used one of the following methods to speak to you—a repeated theme, an impression, a confirmation, a spirit check, or a verse from the Bible. How did you know it was God speaking? (Remember, often it isn't until we've obeyed that we realize it was His voice all along.)

7. What does the statement "The teacher is always silent during a test" mean to you (especially in light of the story of Jesus and the three praying women told on pages 116–17)?

8. What spoke most to you in this chapter?

CHAPTER EIGHT: UNWINDING GRAVECLOTHES

Questions for Discussion or Reflection

1. Read the story of the good Samaritan in Luke 10:30–35. Based on your nature, if you had been on the road that day, which of the following roles might you have played? (I've embellished a bit!)
   - The Priest—saw the bruised and bleeding man but kept moving, too busy to stop.
   - The Levite—looked closer but didn't feel adequate to help so dialed 911 as he went on his way.
   - The Soccer Mom—was distracted by squabbling kids and text messages and didn't even notice.
   - The Samaritan—laid aside his plans and got involved, helping the wounded man.
   - Other: _____

2. Read "Kissing Frogs" on page 124. It has been said that we should love people when they least expect it and least deserve it. Think of a time when someone loved you like that—or a time when you had the privilege of doing that for someone else. Describe the experience.

Going Deeper

3. Read 1 John 3:16–20 and answer the following questions:
    - According to verse 16, who is our example, and what did He do?
    - What warning are we given in verse 17?
    - Instead of offering words and lip service, how are we to love (verse 18)?
    - What amazing benefit (verses 19–20) do we derive from loving like that?

4. Which of the "Lessons from Good Sam" (pages 132–33) speaks most to you? Which seems the most challenging? Why?

5. Do you have a friend or acquaintance who is struggling to escape graveclothes right now? Take a moment to pray for her or him. Ask what God would have you do to help love that person back to life. (It may be as simple as a phone call, a shared meal, or an encouraging note.) Whatever He lays on your heart, do it—knowing that God wants to love that person through you.

6. While we've discussed how we can help others unwind their graveclothes, what does Hebrews 12:1–6 tell us about unwinding our own? List at least five things we should do.

7. Read Isaiah 64:6 and Revelation 3:17. How does our insistence on wearing the "filthy rags" of our own righteousness keep us from experiencing true healing and freedom? According to Revelation 3:18–19, what does God "counsel" us to do?

8. What spoke most to you in this chapter?

Chapter Nine: Living Resurrected

Questions for Discussion or Reflection

1. Have you ever witnessed an amazing transformation in someone's life that was brought about by Christ? Describe it. How did seeing it make you feel?

2. If you were asked to give a testimony of transformation in your life, what would you say? If you can't think of one, is there an attitude or behavior you are currently asking the Lord to change? Describe the difference you believe it will make when this aspect of your life is transformed.

Going Deeper

3. Complete Jesus's seven "I am" sayings listed below. Circle the one that currently means the most to you and explain why.

    John 6:35   "I am the bread of life _____."

    John 8:12   "I am the light of the world _____."

    John 10:9   "I am the gate _____."

    John 10:14–15   "I am the good shepherd _____."

    John 11:25   "I am the resurrection and the life _____."

    John 14:6   "I am the way and the truth and the life _____."

    John 15:5   "I am the vine _____."

4. Knowing the "Great I Am" (Jesus Himself) helps us better understand who we are as well. Look at Appendix D: "Who I Am in Christ." Choose one phrase from each of the three categories, and write out the corresponding verse. Memorize one to include in your Holy Spirit "knowledge base."

5. List three things that currently "move you"—make you overreact or feel upset, worried, and/or fearful. Now describe how counting yourself dead (Romans 6:11) might help change your perspective and enable you to say along with Paul, "nor did I count my life dear to myself" (Acts 20:24, NKJV). If applicable, name a time in your life when your relationship with Christ helped change your lower nature reaction.

6. Meditate on John 15:1–8. Read it several times, and allow the verses to penetrate your heart. Circle or underline phrases that have particular meaning for you. In the context of these verses, what is the difference between striving and abiding? In practical terms, what would choosing to abide actually look like in your life? What would have to change?

7. Read George Müller's secret of service on page 151. Using it as a template, write an obituary for yourself, declaring your decision to die so that Christ might live.

8. What spoke most to you in this chapter?

Chapter Ten: Laughing Lazarus

Questions for Discussion or Reflection

1. Have you ever escaped a dangerous, life-threatening situation? Describe it and the emotions you felt after cheating death. If you've never actually experienced this, describe how you think you would feel.

2. Read the "Living in the Light of Eternity" sidebar on page 168. What aspect of living resurrected would you like to begin practicing right now? What single change in your life would help you do this?

Going Deeper

3. If you really believed that this world isn't all there is, how would it affect the way you view the following aspects of your life? (Write your response first, then consider the scripture given.)

Finances: _____
(Matthew 6:19–21)
Worries: _____
(2 Corinthians 4:17–18)

Sickness: _____

(2 Corinthians 12:7–9)

Hardships: _____

(James 1:12)

Persecution: _____

(John 15:18–20)

4. Which of the following myths have you been able to discard as you've studied the story of Lazarus? Place a check mark (✓) by those you've let go of and a question mark (?) by the ones you'd like to let go of. Feel free to add any other myths about God's love you have become aware of.

_____ We must earn God's favor.

_____ If God loves us, terrible things should never happen to us.

_____ Death is the worst thing possible.

_____ God is distant when we suffer.

_____ God's timing really stinks.

_____ Tragedy is just tragedy—nothing good can come of it.

_____ Other: _____

5. What do the following verses tell us about Jesus's return and the importance of being ready?

Luke 12:35–37 _____

1 Thessalonians 5:1–6 _____

2 Peter 3:4, 8–14 _____

6. Jesus promised that He would come back to take us to heaven so we could be together with Him (John 14:1–3). In light of that reality, consider the following questions:

• What do you imagine that day will be like?

• How close to Jesus do you hope to be?

• Spiritually, what do you need to begin doing here on earth so that when that day comes, you can be known there as you are known here (1 Corinthians 13:12)?

7. Please don't rush through this last exercise. Take time to allow the truth of the following hymn, "The Love of God," to move from your head to your heart. Read the words slowly, then say or sing them again. Allow the immensity of the Father's love to wash over your heart. Rest in it. Revel in it. Receive it as truth. Then write a prayer asking the Holy Spirit to make God's love real in every corner of your heart.

> The love of God is greater far
> Than tongue or pen can ever tell;
> It goes beyond the highest star,
> And reaches to the lowest hell;
> The guilty pair, bowed down with care,
> God gave His Son to win;
> His erring child He reconciled,
> And pardoned from his sin.
>
> *Refrain:*
> O love of God, how rich and pure!
> How measureless and strong!
> It shall forevermore endure
> The saints' and angels' song.
>
> When years of time shall pass away,
> And earthly thrones and kingdoms fall,
> When men, who here refuse to pray,
> On rocks and hills and mountains call,
> God's love so sure, shall still endure,
> All measureless and strong;
> Redeeming grace to Adam's race—
> The saints' and angels' song.
>
> Could we with ink the ocean fill,
> And were the skies of parchment made,

Were every stalk on earth a quill,

And every man a scribe by trade,

To write the love of God above,

Would drain the ocean dry.

Nor could the scroll contain the whole,

Though stretched from sky to sky.

—Frederick M. Lehman[2]

8. Looking back on your journey through this book, what concept has made the biggest impact on you? In what ways has it changed the way you think or live, especially in the area of love-doubt?

Using This Study in an Eight-Week Format

Because this is a shorter study than the ones in my other two books, it may fit well at the end of a Bible-study year or as a summer study. If ten weeks is too long for what you have in mind, you can adapt it to the number of weeks you need by combining chapters (though I would discourage doing fewer than eight sessions).

While you are free to choose how to combine chapters, I suggest covering chapters 1 and 2 ("Tale of the Third Follower" and "Lord, the One You Love Is Sick") in your opening week and chapters 9 and 10 ("Living Resurrected" and "Laughing Lazarus") in your last week of study. When combining weeks, choose one "For Discussion or Reflection" question from each chapter and three from each "Going Deeper" section. Be sure to assign these selected questions the week before the chapters are to be discussed.

As I mentioned at the beginning of this guide, you'll find even more Bible-study resources on my Web site: www.joannaweaverbooks.com. The "Going Deeper/ Book Study Helps" section features a reproducible study guide in a workbook format and a leader's guide. After you've finished your study, please visit the site again to share creative ideas of what worked well for you. I look forward to hearing them!

Resources for Resurrected Living

Never before have there been so many resources available to help Christians live resurrected, grasp God's love better, and learn to be His friend. While nothing replaces the Word of God, the Holy Spirit often speaks through other avenues as well. Here are some books and resources that have really helped me.

GETTING GOD'S LOVE FROM YOUR HEAD TO YOUR HEART

The Rabbi's Heartbeat by Brennan Manning. Colorado Springs, CO: NavPress, 2003. This truly beautiful devotional offers everyday challenges and encouragement to accept your identity as God's beloved child.

The Tender Words of God: A Daily Guide by Ann Spangler. Grand Rapids: Zondervan, 2008. This very personal devotional uses Scripture to help you develop a deeper sense of being loved by God.

Love Beyond Reason: Moving God's Love from Your Head to Your Heart by John Ortberg. Grand Rapids: Zondervan, 1998. This encouraging book reveals a Father who is head over heels in love with His children and committed to their highest joy.

Waking the Dead: The Glory of a Heart Fully Alive by John Eldredge. Nashville: Thomas Nelson, 2003. Eldredge's powerful book shows how to energize your life by living—really living—from the heart.

What's So Amazing About Grace? by Philip Yancey. Grand Rapids: Zondervan, 2002. This modern classic focuses on the transforming—and love-doubt erasing—power of grace in our lives.

Do You Think I'm Beautiful?: The Question Every Woman Asks by Angela Thomas. Nashville: Thomas Nelson, 2005. This warm, reassuring book invites women to meet the embrace of the One who calls them beautiful.

Crazy Love: Overwhelmed by a Relentless God by Francis Chan. Colorado Springs, CO: David C. Cook, 2008. Chan provides a fresh and compelling exploration of God's radical, relentless, "crazy" love for us—and how we can respond.

BEING A FRIEND OF GOD

My Utmost for His Highest by Oswald Chambers. This Christian classic, originally published in 1935, remains fresh and challenging. My edition is from Barbour Books, but an updated-language version is available from Discovery House. You can also access daily readings of this classic work on the Internet at www .myutmost.org.

Streams in the Desert and *Springs in the Valley* by Lettie B. (Mrs. Charles) Cowman. These inspirational compilations first appeared in 1925 and 1939 respectively and are still popular today. I own them in a combined edition. James Reimann edited updated-language versions, which are available from Zondervan.

The Indwelling Life of Christ: All of Him in All of Me by Major W. Ian Thomas. Colorado Springs, CO: Multnomah Publishers, 2006. This devotional—one of my personal favorites—reminds me that the secret of living a transformed life is letting Jesus do the work!

A Call to Die: A 40 Day Journey of Fasting from the World and Feasting on God by David Nasser. Birmingham, AL: Redemptive Art Publishing, 2000. Complete with daily questions and action plans, this remarkable devotional is basically a hands-on workbook on dying to self.

Jesus Calling: Enjoying Peace in His Presence by Sarah Young. Nashville: Thomas, Nelson, 2004. This devotional—a classic in the making—grew out of Sarah Young's prayer journals. Written as if in the voice of Jesus, it speaks words of peace and comfort with remarkable intimacy and immediacy.

The Pursuit of God by A. W. Tozer. Camp Hill, PA: WingSpread, 1992. First published in 1948 and still in print, this perennial classic explores the in-depth implications of knowing Christ, and it challenges me every time I read it.

Discerning the Voice of God: How to Recognize When God Speaks by Priscilla Shirer. Chicago: Moody, 2007. Using biblical principles and practical insights from saints, both current and past, Shirer helps us tune in to God's voice. (The author's six-week DVD teaching series is also available on the subject: *He Speaks to Me: Preparing to Hear from God.* Nashville: LifeWay, 2005.)

GETTING OUT OF YOUR TOMB

One Day at a Time: The Devotional for Overcomers by Neil T. Anderson, Mike and Julia Quarles. Ventura, CA: Regal, 2000. Based on Dr. Anderson's *Steps to Freedom in Christ* recovery model, this devotional provides daily encouragement for anyone struggling with sin, addiction, obsession, and depression. (For more about Dr. Anderson's Freedom in Christ ministry, see his Web site: www.ficm .org/newsite/index.php.)

Get Out of That Pit: Straight Talk about God's Deliverance by Beth Moore. Nashville: Integrity, 2007. America's favorite Bible teacher offers fresh understanding on the pits—or tombs—we get ourselves into and how to find freedom through Christ.

Praying God's Word: Breaking Free from Spiritual Strongholds by Beth Moore. Nashville: Broadman and Holman, 2000. This prayer guide examines fourteen strongholds that entomb Christians and suggests scriptures to help demolish them through daily prayer.

Breaking Free: Making Liberty in Christ a Reality in Life DVD series and workbook by Beth Moore. Nashville: LifeWay Christian Resources, 2006. All Beth Moore studies are good, but this one is a personal favorite. It includes eleven weeks of DVD teaching for groups and individual Bible study. An updated series is available under the title *Breaking Free: The Journey, The Stories.*

The Search for Significance: Seeing Your True Worth through God's Eyes by Robert S. McGee. Rev. ed. Nashville: W Publishing Group, 2003. "Approval addicts" like me and those hung up on performance, blame, and other "self-disorders" will find help in this classic reminder that our true value is found in Christ.

Lord, I Want to Be Whole: The Power of Prayer and Scripture in Emotional Healing by Stormie Omartian. Nashville: Thomas Nelson, 2000. For those who struggle with anger, guilt, and depression, Stormie Omartian offers seven biblical steps to wholeness.

Lies Women Believe: And the Truth That Sets Them Free by Nancy Leigh DeMoss. Chicago: Moody, 2001. DeMoss exposes areas of deception we commonly fall for—about ourselves, sin, relationships, emotions, and circumstances—and shows how confronting these lies can help set us free.

Celebrate Recovery. Based on eight principles from the Beatitudes, this program was begun at Pastor Rick Warren's Saddleback Church and offers a number of Christ-centered resources to help those struggling with sin and addiction—media, resource kits, conferences, and access to support groups throughout the country. Check out the Web site at www.celebraterecovery.com.

A Hunger for Healing: The Twelve Steps as a Classic Model for Christian Spiritual Growth by J. Keith Miller. New York: HarperOne, 1992. This book, too, has become something of a classic and powerfully applies the Twelve Steps of Alcoholics Anonymous not only to addictions but to growing closer to Christ.

OTHER RESOURCES

Christianity.com (www.christianity.com). This is a one-stop source for Bible study, devotionals, articles, blogs—you name it.

Bible Study Tools: Growing Deeper in the Word (www.biblestudytools.com). This site offers commentaries, Bible study helps, and the like.

Bible Gateway (www.biblegateway.com). The site provides easy access to the most popular (and some obscure) Bible translations and allows searches by verse or keyword.

Christian Classics Ethereal Library (www.ccel.org). Most of the great public-domain Christian classics can be found here and read online or downloaded in several different formats.

Christianity Today International (www.christianitytoday.com). This site hosts a number of excellent magazines, including the online version of *Christianity Today* and the women's magazine *Kyria* (formerly *Today's Christian Woman*).

Focus on the Family (www.focusonthefamily.com). This site provides wonderful resources relating to family, marriage, and spiritual growth.

Who I Am in Christ

E ver since Adam and Eve bit into the forbidden fruit, humanity has struggled with an identity crisis. We've forgotten who we really are—chosen and beloved children of God. Consider the following list of scriptures from the wonderful devotional *One Day at a Time*.[1]

I Am Accepted

John 1:12	I am God's child.
John 15:15	I am Christ's friend.
Romans 5:1	I have been justified.
1 Corinthians 6:17	I am united with the Lord, and I am one spirit with Him.
1 Corinthians 6:20	I have been bought with a price. I belong to God.
1 Corinthians12:27	I am a member of Christ's body.
Ephesians 1:1	I am a saint.
Ephesians 1:5	I have been adopted as God's child.
Ephesians 2:18	I have direct access to God through the Holy Spirit.
Colossians 1:14	I have been redeemed and forgiven of all my sins.
Colossians 2:10	I am complete in Christ.

I Am Secure

Romans 8:1–2	I am free from condemnation.
Romans 8:28	I am assured that all things work together for good.

Romans 8:31–34	I am free from any condemning charges against me.
Romans 8:35–39	I cannot be separated from the love of God.
2 Corinthians 1:21–22	I have been established, anointed, and sealed by God.
Colossians 3:3	I am hidden with Christ in God.
Philippians 1:6	I am confident that the good work God has begun in me will be perfected.
Philippians 3:20	I am a citizen of heaven.
2 Timothy 1:7	I have not been given a spirit of fear but of power, love, and a sound mind.
Hebrews 4:16	I can find grace and mercy to help in time of need.
1 John 5:18	I am born of God, and the evil one cannot touch me.

I Am Significant

Matthew 5:13–14	I am the salt and light of the earth.
John 15:1, 5	I am a branch of the true vine, a channel of His life.
John 15:16	I have been chosen and appointed to bear fruit.
Acts 1:8	I am a personal witness of Christ.
1 Corinthians 3:16	I am God's temple.
2 Corinthians 5:17–21	I am a minister of reconciliation for God.
2 Corinthians 6:1	I am God's co-worker (see 1 Corinthians 3:9).
Ephesians 2:6	I am seated with Christ in the heavenly realm.
Ephesians 2:10	I am God's workmanship.
Ephesians 3:12	I may approach God with freedom and confidence.
Philippians 4:13	I can do all things through Christ, who strengthens me.

Identifying Strongholds

A stronghold, remember, is a hurt, a habit, or a hang-up that keeps us entombed, unable to live freely and fully. Strongholds may involve false beliefs, established attitudes, and compulsive behavior patterns, including addictions. Some are inherently harmful (like smoking), while others may only be a problem if they become entrenched in your life and hold you back from freedom. The following questions may help you recognize tombs that are hemming you in, shutting you down, or closing you off:

1. *Do you struggle with "repeated, unwanted behavior"?*[1] You may find yourself doing things you don't want to do or struggling with negative or destructive thought patterns. This behavior is so engrained it is nearly second nature, though you know it isn't right. It can be anything from anger to chronic laziness, violent reactions to habitual lying—to name just a few.

2. *Do you tend to turn to this behavior or thought pattern when things are difficult or you feel depressed?* It may offer a strong (but false) sense of comfort and initially make you feel better, even though you know it's not good for you. Whether it's compulsive shopping; mental escapism through television, reading, or the Internet; overeating; pornography; alcohol; or something else—your first impulse when troubled is to turn to it rather than to God.

3. *Do you have difficulty understanding why you react to certain things the way you do?* Certain experiences may trigger overreactions that don't fit the situation. The strength of the emotion surprises even you, but you can't seem to help yourself. Watch out for tendencies toward verbal retaliation, extreme anger and defensiveness, paranoia, or self-hatred.

4. *Do you have a secret no one knows?* Shame from your past or "family business" that you've been warned not to talk about can haunt your present life and keep you from connecting with people in meaningful ways. Secrets and shame can lead to emotional paralysis, shyness, isolation, cynicism, or a chameleon tendency to role-play rather than be real.

5. *Do you find yourself stuck somewhere in your past or stalled in the grief process?* You may find yourself longing to go back to a certain point in your life or continually reliving a painful event. You may simmer with anger over a long-ago injustice or feel paralyzed by grief over a significant loss. There's nothing wrong with a bit of nostalgia, and needing time to heal after trauma or loss is normal and necessary. But ongoing and unresolved feelings about the past can eventually harden into strongholds.

6. *Do you have an unsubstantiated and intense dislike of a certain type or group of people*—men, women, liberals or conservatives, corporate types, Muslims, Jews, tattooed Norwegians? Any contact with the group—or simply thinking about them—may inspire deep discomfort, fear, anger, or even hatred. Making sweeping judgments and assumptions about individual members of the group without actually getting to know them is a telltale sign as well.

7. *Do you accept your limitations as your definition?* This could mean you've allowed demeaning words from the past to define you: "I'm not athletic... or talented..." "I probably won't amount to anything." You may frequently use the excuse "That's just the way I am" to deflect blame or responsibility for your behavior or your reactions: "I always lose my temper because I'm Italian/Greek/Irish" or "In our family we just don't do feelings."

8. *Do you get offended when other people point out unhealthy behaviors that you don't (or do!) see in yourself?* Defensiveness is usually a sign that we've come in contact with some kind of truth. If more than one person suggests you have a problem, it makes sense to listen, even if you're sure they're wrong. Don't underestimate the power of denial to keep you in bondage. Ask God to help you see what you need to see.

If you have recognized yourself in any of the questions above, the first step toward finding freedom is to bring the situation before God. Here are some suggestions for how to do that:

- Give God specific permission to shine the spotlight of the Holy Spirit on your soul.
- Follow the Reveal-Repent-Renounce-Replace outline suggested in the "Dethroning Lies" sidebar on pages 76–77.
- Ask God to show you what He would have you do next in order to live free. Don't forget to deal with the lies of unworthiness, unforgiveness, and unbelief that may also play a part in your bondage.
- Allow the Holy Spirit to direct your path as you seek further counseling, prayer support, and perhaps a recovery group that addresses your specific need.

Hints for Unwinding Graveclothes

While only God can resurrect dead people, He specifically calls us to help love them back into life. Although chapter 8 already covered a lot of information about unwinding graveclothes, here are some extra tips I've picked up over the years:

1. *Be available (Matthew 9:36).* Ask for eyes to see what God sees and where He would have you participate in His work. When you recognize a need, ask how He wants you to be involved. Sometimes prayer is our only calling. But when the Holy Spirit prompts you to step forward into the situation, don't shrink back.

2. *Pray specifically about what God is calling you to do (Isaiah 30:21).* Whether it involves taking an hour to listen or a significant ongoing investment of time and resources—whatever you feel called to do, do it. But also check your motives. Keep in mind that the work is God's, and you are simply there to do what He tells you.

3. *Listen to the person's story (Galatians 6:2).* Too often we operate out of faulty assumptions. Ask the person to share his or her story, and insert pertinent questions to help the process along. Often it isn't until we know where people have been that we're able to help them get where they need to be—and the very act of listening brings healing. At the same time, don't allow yourself to get swept into an emotional drama and forget to factor in God.

4. *Be trustworthy (Proverbs 11:13).* When a person tells you something in confidence, don't share it elsewhere without permission—not even in vague prayer requests or in general, unnamed discussions. Be a safe haven in which other people can learn to trust and rest their hearts. (Note: The only exception to the confidentiality rule is in cases of abuse, imminent danger, or suicidal tendencies. These must be reported, but let the person involved know you are going to do so.)

5. *Invite Jesus into the interaction (James 5:16).* You'll want to do this with care and sensitivity, as some have been wounded by religious people in the past. (Sadly, it happens.) Look for ways to bring Jesus and His love into the conversation in nonjudgmental ways. Pray together, taking each and every need to Him. Encourage the development of a personal relationship with God, and gently urge the other person to turn to Him first with his or her needs.

6. *Ask God for wisdom (Colossians 1:9).* Let the Bible be your guide. Don't counsel solely out of your own experience, opinion, or bias, or you may give tainted advice. Ask the Holy Spirit for a gift of faith to see what the person can become so that you minister out of hope, not despair. Find scriptural promises to pray and declare boldly over the person's life. Ask the Lord to lead you to helpful resources you can share.

7. *Speak the truth in love (Ephesians 4:15).* Someone has said, "Love without truth is flattery, but truth without love is cruelty." Ask God to give you a genuine love for the person. Speak words of affirmation often, pointing out good qualities in his or her life and praising the progress made. But don't be afraid to gently point out inconsistencies between the person's life and God's Word. Do it humbly and gently, knowing that truth sets us free.

8. *Make room for others to help (Proverbs 15:22).* We are rarely the only ones God uses in people's lives. God has also appointed certain people—parents, spouses, pastors—to provide both authority and spiritual protection. Honor and support such "coverings" when appropriate. Be willing to decrease so other godly influences can increase. If you sense the other person is becoming overly dependent on you, point it out gently and slowly step back so

God can step in. And don't be offended if your season in someone's life comes to an end sooner than you think it should.

9. *Remember, graveclothes consist of layers (Galatians 6:9–10).* Freedom doesn't come all at once. It is a process of healing you are witnessing, not an event. Don't give way to cynicism or frustration when it seems to take longer than it should or when one problem is dealt with only to reappear in another form. Encourage yourself and the one you minister to that God will be faithful to finish what He has started. We simply have to cooperate—one layer at a time.

10. *Above all, trust God (Hebrews 12:2).* Lasting healing is God's work, and He's good at it. Trust that the Holy Spirit is working in the heart of the one who needs freedom, and let Him have His way in you as well. Be willing to do what God asks when He asks it, then commit the person to His love and His care. Operate out of faith, not fear. Then watch what God will do!

Notes

Epigraph

Quoted in Dan Clendenin, "Ancient Wisdom for the Modern World: My New Year's Resolutions with Help from the Desert Monastics," *Journey with Jesus,* January 1, 2006, www.journeywithjesus.net/Essays/20051226JJ.shtml. Adapted from John Chryssavgis's translation in *In the Heart of the Desert: The Spirituality of the Desert Fathers and Mothers,* rev. ed. (Bloomington, IN: World Wisdom, 2008), 1.

Chapter One: Tale of the Third Follower

1. Anna B. Warner, "Jesus Loves Me," first published in Anna B. Warner and Susan Warner, *Say and Seal* (Philadelphia: Lippincott, 1860), 115–16.
2. For the full story of Martha and Mary and the way they grew in relationship to Jesus, see my books, *Having a Mary Heart in a Martha World: Finding Intimacy with God in the Busyness of Life* (Colorado Springs, CO: WaterBrook, 2000, 2002) and *Having a Mary Spirit: Allowing God to Change Us from the Inside Out* (Colorado Springs, CO: WaterBrook, 2006).
3. Bono, in Michka Assayas, *Bono: In Conversation with Michka Assayas* (New York: Penguin, Berkley, 2006), 225.
4. Bono, in Assayas, *Bono: In Conversation,* 226.
5. For an enlightening discussion of the tendency toward "will worship," see Richard J. Foster, *Celebration of Discipline: The Path to Spiritual Growth,* rev. ed. (1978; repr., San Francisco: HarperSanFrancisco, 1988), 5–6.

Chapter Two: Lord, the One You Love Is Sick

1. Commenting on the time line of Lazarus's sickness, Warren Wiersbe writes: "Jesus was at Bethabara, about twenty miles from Bethany.... If the [messenger] had traveled quickly, without any delay, he could have made the trip in one day. Jesus sent him back the next day... Then Jesus waited two more

days…and by the time He and His disciples arrived, Lazarus had been dead for four days. This means that Lazarus had died *the very day* the messenger left to contact Jesus!" In Warren W. Wiersbe, *Be Alive* (Colorado Springs, CO: David C. Cook, 1981), 132.

2. According to the *NIV Study Bible* notes on John 9:2, "The rabbis had developed the principle that 'There is no death without sin, and there is no suffering without iniquity.' They were even capable of thinking that a child could sin in the womb or that its soul might have sinned in a preexistent state. They also held that terrible punishments came on certain people because of the sin of their parents. As the next verse [John 9:3] shows, Jesus plainly contradicted these beliefs." Kenneth L. Barker, ed., *The NIV Study Bible,* 10th anniversary ed. (Grand Rapids: Zondervan, 1995).

3. Jerry Goebel, "Unbind Him and Let Him Go!" ONEFamily Outreach, March 13, 2005, http://onefamilyoutreach.com/bible/John/jn_11_01-45 .htm.

4. Adapted from Rosalind Goforth, *Climbing: Memories of a Missionary's Wife,* 2nd ed. (1940; repr., Elkhart, IN: Bethel, 1996), 80.

5. *Steps to Peace with God* (Charlotte, NC: Billy Graham Evangelistic Association, n.d.), www.billygraham.org/specialsections/steps-to-peace/steps-to-peace.asp.

6. After much study I've come to believe we are three-part beings, as referred to by Paul in 1 Thessalonians 5:23: "May God himself, the God of peace, sanctify you through and through. May your whole spirit, soul and body be kept blameless at the coming of our Lord Jesus Christ." The "body" is the physical shell that houses us; the "soul" is our mind, will, and emotions; and the "spirit" is the place that comes alive when Christ takes up residence within us at salvation. For a deeper discussion on this topic and why I believe the distinction is important, see *Having a Mary Spirit: Allowing God to Change Us from the Inside Out* (beginning with chapter 2).

7. Quoted in Dale Fincher, "A Slice of Infinity: What Do You Expect? Part 5," Ravi Zacharias International Ministries, January 30, 2004, www.rzim.org/resources/read/asliceofinfinity/todaysslice.aspx?aid=8420.

8. Quoted in John Eldredge, *Waking the Dead: The Glory of a Heart Fully Alive* (Nashville: Thomas Nelson, 2003), 75.

Chapter Three: Our Friend Lazarus

1. James Strong, *The New Strong's Exhaustive Concordance of the Bible* (Nashville: Thomas Nelson, 1996), s.v. "#1690."
2. David Giles, *Illusions of Immortality: A Psychology of Fame and Celebrity* (London: Macmillan, 2000), 95.
3. Giles, *Illusions of Immortality*, 95.
4. Francis Chan, *Crazy Love: Overwhelmed by a Relentless God* (Colorado Springs, CO: David C. Cook, 2008), 110–11.
5. Gene Edwards, *The Divine Romance* (1984; repr., Wheaton, IL: Tyndale, 1992), 63–64.
6. Max Lucado, *God Came Near* (1986; repr., Nashville: Thomas Nelson, 2004), 56.
7. Spiros Zodhiates, gen. ed., *The Complete Word Study Dictionary: New Testament*, rev. ed. (Chattanooga, TN: AMG International, 1993), s.v. "#2083."
8. Zodhiates, *Complete Word Study Dictionary*, s.v. "#2083."
9. Zodhiates, *Complete Word Study Dictionary*, s.v. "#2083."
10. Zodhiates, *Complete Word Study Dictionary*, s.v. "#2083."
11. C. H. Spurgeon, "The Friend of God," *The Homiletic Review*, vol. 14, no. 1 (July–December 1887), 157.
12. George Müller to J. Hudson Taylor, in Dr. and Mrs. Howard Taylor, *Hudson Taylor's Spiritual Secret*, Moody Classics ed. (Chicago: Moody, 2009), 152–53.
13. Joseph C. Ludgate, "Friendship with Jesus," in *Hymns of Glorious Praise* (Springfield, MO: Gospel Publishing, 1969), 338.

Chapter Four: When Love Tarries

1. *Dark Night of the Soul* was originally the title of a poem and an accompanying commentary by Spanish mystic and Carmelite friar Saint John of the Cross (1542–1591).

2. Brian Jones, *Second Guessing God: Hanging On When You Can't See His Plan* (Cincinnati, OH: Standard Publishing, 2006), 13.

3. Jones, *Second Guessing God,* 15.

4. Jones, *Second Guessing God,* 15.

5. Jones, *Second Guessing God,* 15.

6. Pastor Don Burleson, "Big T-Truth" (sermon, New Covenant Fellowship, Kalispell, MT, June 8, 2008).

7. Warren Wiersbe, *The Wiersbe Bible Commentary: Old Testament,* 2nd ed. (Colorado Springs, CO: David C. Cook, 2007), 755. Emphasis in scriptures and outline format are mine.

8. Charles H. Spurgeon, "A Mystery! Saints Sorrowing and Jesus Glad!" (sermon no. 585, Metropolitan Tabernacle, Newington, England, August 7, 1864), quoted in *Spurgeon's Sermons,* vol. 10: 1864, Christian Classics Ethereal Library, http://153.106.5.3/ccel/spurgeon/sermons10.xviii.html.

9. According to the *NIV Study Bible* notes on John 11:17, "Many Jews believed that the soul remained near the body for three days after death in the hope of returning to it. If this idea was in the minds of these people, they obviously thought all hope was gone—Lazarus was irrevocably dead." Kenneth L. Barker, ed., *The NIV Study Bible,* 10th anniversary ed. (Grand Rapids: Zondervan, 1995).

10. Jerry Goebel, "Unbind Him and Let Him Go!" ONEFamily Outreach, March 13, 2005, http://onefamilyoutreach.com/bible/John/jn_11_01-45.htm.

11. Perhaps you've wondered, as I have, what Jesus meant when He addressed the disciples' concerns about returning to Bethany by saying, "Are there not twelve hours of daylight?" (John 11:9). Ray Stedman writes, "He is referring to the appointed timetable of God... He was determined to walk in the daylight of God's will. To step out of that timetable—even if doing so would *seem* safer by human reasoning—would be tantamount to walking by night. It would lead to stumbling.... God has appointed a time for each of us, and... there is nothing anyone else can do to shorten it, nor is there anything we can do to lengthen it. Our times are in God's hands." Ray C. Stedman with James D. Denney, *God's Loving Word: Exploring the Gospel of John* (Grand Rapids: Discovery House, 1993), 298.

12. I first heard David's story years ago on a recording from a talk he had given. I have since contacted him personally and received both his confirmation that the material is accurate and his permission to use it. For more on David Ring's Reach Out and Touch ministries, visit his Web site: www.davidring.org.

13. Not his real name

14. Thanks to Martha Tennison for this phrase, which I heard in a sermon delivered in Billings, Montana, September 24, 1999.

Chapter Five: Tomb Dwelling

1. [Matthew] Henry and [Thomas] Scott, *A Commentary upon the Holy Bible, Matthew to Acts* (London: Religious Tract Society, 1835), 54 n. 28.

2. "Bethany: Meeting Place for Friends," Franciscan Cyberspot, http://198.62.75.1/www1/ofm/san/BET09mod.html.

3. "The Ossuary of James," The Nazarene Way, www.thenazareneway.com/ossuary_of_james.htm.

4. While the "hurts, hang-ups, and habits" phrase was coined by Rick Warren and John E. Baker and is used extensively in the Celebrate Recovery organization, the descriptions of the three kinds of strongholds are mine. For more about Celebrate Recovery, which I highly recommend, please see Appendix C: "Resources for Resurrected Living."

5. This description is taken from John Baker, *Celebrate Recovery® Leader's Guide,* updated ed. (Grand Rapids: Zondervan, 2005), 56.

6. This information was collected from a four-year (and ongoing) survey of more than 200 churches conducted by the REVEAL™ research and strategy initiative under the auspices of the Willow Creek Association ministry. See Greg Hawkins and Cally Parkinson, *Follow Me: What's Next for You* (South Barrington, IL: Willow Creek Resources, 2008), 100.

7. Spiros Zodhiates, gen. ed., *The Complete Word Study Dictionary: New Testament,* rev. ed. (Chattanooga, TN: AMG International, 1993), s.v. "#3415" and "#3418."

8. Rick Renner, *Sparkling Gems from the Greek: 365 Greek Word Studies for Every Day of the Year to Sharpen Your Understanding of God's Word* (Tulsa, OK: Teach All Nations, 2003), 74.

Chapter Six: Roll Away the Stone

1. This is actually the subtitle of Groeschel's excellent book *The Christian Atheist: Believing in God but Living As If He Doesn't Exist* (Grand Rapids: Zondervan, 2010).

2. Joyce Meyer, *Battlefield of the Mind: Winning the Battle in Your Mind* (1995; repr., New York: Warner Faith, 2002), 12.

3. Ann Spangler, *The Tender Words of God: A Daily Guide* (Grand Rapids: Zondervan, 2008), 13.

4. Spangler, *Tender Words of God,* 15–16.

5. Spangler, *Tender Words of God,* 14.

6. Kenneth Wuest, *Wuest's Word Studies from the Greek New Testament,* vol. 2 (Grand Rapids: Eerdmans, 1973), 121.

7. The Greek word *dunamis* is used in the Bible to describe God's "miraculous power." (See James Strong, *The New Strong's Exhaustive Concordance of the Bible* (Nashville: Thomas Nelson, 1996), s.v. "1411, dunamis." It is also the root of our English word *dynamite.* (See "Word History," *American Heritage Dictionary of the English Language,* 4th ed., s.v. "dynamite," http://dictionary .reference.com/browse/dynamite.

Chapter Seven: When Love Calls Your Name

1. This phrase is inspired by the great hymn "Come Thou Fount of Every Blessing," whose words were written by Robert Robinson in 1758. For the story of how it was written, see "Come Thou Fount of Every Blessing," Center for Church Music Songs and Hymns, http://songsandhymns.org/hymns/ detail/come-thou-fount-of-every-blessing.

2. Priscilla Shirer, *Discerning the Voice of God: How to Recognize When God Speaks* (Chicago: Moody, 2007), 14.

3. Philip Yancey, *Grace Notes: Daily Readings with a Fellow Pilgrim* (Grand Rapids: Zondervan, 2009), 168.

4. Ken Gire, *Reflections on Your Life Journal: Discerning God's Voice in the Everyday Moments of Life* (Colorado Springs, CO: Chariot Victor, 1998), 11–12.

5. Henri J. M. Nouwen, *Letters to Marc About Jesus: Living a Spiritual Life in a Material World,* trans. Hubert Hoskins (San Francisco: HarperSanFrancisco, 1998), 84.

6. Brother Lawrence (ca. 1614–1691) was a French Carmelite lay brother whose simplicity and great wisdom inspired many during his life. After Lawrence's death, Father Joseph de Beaufort compiled his letters and conversations into a book called *The Practice of the Presence of God,* now considered a Christian classic. See "Biography of Brother Lawrence," Christian Classics Ethereal Library, www.ccel.org/l/Lawrence.

7. For more on journaling, see my book *Having a Mary Heart in a Martha World: Finding Intimacy with God in the Busyness of Life* (Colorado Springs, CO: WaterBrook, 2000), chapter 5 and Appendix D.

8. Special thanks to Marla Campbell, who shared this thought with me many years ago.

9. Shirer, *Discerning the Voice of God,* 184.

10. Oswald Chambers, *My Utmost for His Highest: The Golden Book of Oswald Chambers, Selections for the Year* (1935; repr., Westwood, NJ: Barbour, 1963), January 30.

11. Thanks to Dianne Freitag for this phrase, shared in personal conversation.

12. Mrs. Charles [Lettie B.] Cowman, *Streams in the Desert,* in *Streams in the Desert and Springs in the Valley,* Zondervan Treasures (1925; repr., Grand Rapids: Zondervan, 1996), February 9.

13. Cowman, *Streams in the Desert,* February 9.

Chapter Eight: Unwinding Graveclothes

1. Henry M. Grout, "The Good Samaritan," in The Monday Club, *Sermons on the International Sunday-School Lessons for 1881,* Sixth Series (New York: Thomas Y. Crowell, 1880), 151–2. Note: this passage seems to be a summary of ideas found in Charles H. Spurgeon's sermon "The Good Samaritan," sermon no. 1360 (delivered at the Metropolitan Tabernacle, Newington, England, June 17, 1877), www.spurgeongems.org/vols22-24/chs1360 .pdf.

2. David O. Mears, "The Good Samaritan," in The Monday Club, *Sermons on the International Sunday-School Lessons for 1878* (Boston: Henry Hoyt, 1878), 303.

3. Wes Seeliger, *Faith at Work,* February 1972, 13, quoted in Bruce Larson, *Ask Me to Dance* (Waco, TX: Word Books, 1972), 11–12.

4. Jerry Goebel, "Unbind Him and Let Him Go!" ONEFamily Outreach, March 13, 2005, http://onefamilyoutreach.com/bible/John/jn_11_01-45.htm.

5. Goebel, "Unbind Him."

6. Goebel, "Unbind Him."

7. Thanks to Pastor Danny Stephenson for this thought.

8. Kathryn Spink, *Mother Teresa: A Complete Authorized Biography* (San Francisco: HarperSanFrancisco, 1997), 245.

9. Not her real name.

10. Mrs. Charles [Lettie B.] Cowman, *Springs in the Valley,* in *Streams in the Desert and Springs in the Valley,* Zondervan Treasures (1939; repr., Grand Rapids: Zondervan, 1996), February 22.

11. Oswald Chambers, *My Utmost for His Highest: The Golden Book of Oswald Chambers, Selections for the Year* (1935; repr., Westwood, NJ: Barbour, 1963), March 24.

12. Frank E. Peretti, *Piercing the Darkness* (Westchester, IL: Crossway Books, 1989).

13. Beth Moore, *Further Still: A Collection of Poetry and Vignettes* (Nashville: Broadman and Holman, 2004), 99–104.

14. Warren Wiersbe, *The Wiersbe Bible Commentary: New Testament,* 2nd ed. (Colorado Springs, CO: David C. Cook, 2007), 862.

Chapter Nine: Living Resurrected

1. Story told in V. Raymond Edman, *They Found the Secret: Twenty Transformed Lives That Reveal a Touch of Eternity* (1960; repr., Grand Rapids: Zondervan, 1984), 17–22. This particular quote is from page 18.

2. Edman, *They Found the Secret,* 19.

3. Edman, *They Found the Secret,* 19.

4. Edman, *They Found the Secret,* 17.

5. Edman, *They Found the Secret,* 17.

6. Hannah Whitall Smith, *The Unselfishness of God* (1903; repr., Princeton, NJ: Littlebrook, 1987), 193.

7. Julie Thompson, "Lazarus," in Charles May, ed., *Masterplots II: Short Story Series,* rev. ed. (Pasadena, CA: Salem Press, 2004), Enotes.com, 2006, www.enotes.com/lazarus-leonid-andreyev-salem/lazarus-9620000246.

8. Wendell Berry, quoted in Eugene H. Peterson, *Living the Resurrection: The Risen Christ in Everyday Life* (Colorado Springs, CO: NavPress, 2006), 13.

9. See my book *Having a Mary Spirit: Allowing God to Change Us from the Inside Out* (Colorado Springs, CO: WaterBrook, 2006), chapters 3 and 5.

10. W. Ian Thomas, *The Indwelling Life of Christ* (Sisters, OR: Multnomah, 2006), 151–52.

11. Thomas, *Indwelling Life of Christ,* 127.

12. Arthur T. Pierson, *George Müller of Bristol* (1899; repr., Grand Rapids: Hendrickson, 2008), 383 (emphasis added).

Chapter Ten: Laughing Lazarus

1. Mrs. Winchester's story and details about the house are summarized from "Sarah Winchester: Woman of Mystery" and "Winchester Mystery House™: Beautiful But Bizarre," Winchester Mystery House, www.winchester mysteryhouse.com/SarahWinchester.cfm and www.winchestermysteryhouse .com/thehouse.cfm. The quotation at the end of this paragraph is from Vernon Grounds, "An Inevitable Appointment," *Our Daily Bread,* April 2, 1994, http://odb.org/1994/04/02/an-inevitable-appointment/.

2. Woody Allen, "Afraid Quotes," Said What? www.saidwhat.co.uk/key wordquotes/afraid.

3. "Al-Eizariya," Serving History: World History Served Up Daily, www.serving history.com/topics/Al-Eizariya. (Al-Eizariya means "place of Lazarus.")

4. "Church of Ayios, Lazaros Larnaca," Serving History: World History Served Up Daily, www.servinghistory.com/topics/Church_of_Ayios,_Lazaros _Larnaca.

5. Eastern Orthodox tradition holds that after his resurrection Lazarus fled to Cyprus to escape persecution, was ordained by Paul and Barnabas as the first bishop of Kition (now Larnarca), and died there thirty years later. A competing tradition, now more or less debunked, holds that Lazarus fled with his sisters to Provence, became bishop of Marseilles, and was martyred and buried in what is now France. See Demetrios Serfes, "St. Lazarus the Friend of Christ and First Bishop of Kition, Cyprus," Lives of the Saints, www.serfes.org/lives/stlazarus.htm and Léon Clugnet, "St. Lazarus of Bethany," *The Catholic Encyclopedia*, vol. 9 (New York: Robert Appleton Company, 1910), www.newadvent .org/cathen/09097a.htm.

6. Ray C. Stedman with James D. Denney, *God's Loving Word: Exploring the Gospel of John* (Grand Rapids: Discovery House, 1993), 300.

7. John Claypool, "Easter and the Fear of Death" (program #3030, Chicago Sunday Evening Club, April 19, 1987), *30 Good Minutes,* www.csec.org// csec/sermon/claypool_3030.htm.

8. Mark Buchanan, *Things Unseen* (Sisters, OR: Multnomah, 2002), 43.

9. Marshall Shelley, "Two Minutes to Eternity," *Christianity Today,* May 16, 1994, 25–7, quoted in Buchanan, *Things Unseen,* 43–44.

10. Elisabeth Elliot, *Keep a Quiet Heart* (Ann Arbor, MI: Servant, 1995), 28.

11. Demetrios Serfes, "St. Lazarus the Friend of Christ and First Bishop of Kition, Cyprus," Lives of the Saints, www.serfes.org/lives/stlazarus.htm.

Appendix B: Study Guide

1. June Shaputis, "Funny Stones to Tickle Your Funny Bones," www.webpanda .com/ponder/epitaphs.htm.

2. Frederick Lehman, "The Love of God," 1917. Lehman wrote this hymn in Pasadena, California, and it was first published in *Songs That Are Different,* vol. 2 (1919). The lyrics are based on the Jewish poem "Haddamut," written in Aramaic in 1050 by Meir Ben Isaac Nehorai, a cantor in Worms, Germany. They have been translated into at least eighteen languages. See www .cyberhymnal.org/htm/l/o/loveofgo.htm.

Appendix D: Who I Am in Christ

1. From *One Day at a Time: The Devotional for Overcomers* by Neil T. Anderson and Mike and Julia Quarles, copyright 2000. Used by permission of Regal Books, a division of Gospel Light Publications. All rights reserved.

Appendix E: Identifying Strongholds

1. Brian Tome, *Free Book* (Nashville: Thomas Nelson, 2010). Tome's chapter on strongholds served as a springboard for some items on this list, but the specific applications and descriptions are mine.

Dear Reader,

After spending an initial year of mental silence while searching for inspiration for this book, I'm amazed at how many more things my heart wants to say as it comes to a close. I keep discovering new facets of the story of Lazarus—ideas and shades of meaning that, along with the ones in this book, can literally change our lives and help us find our place in the heart of God if we'll allow them to do so.

I pray that the Holy Spirit has taken my limited words and breathed fresh revelation to your heart between every line, shaping an individual message that has met your particular need. Helping you to die to yourself daily so that Jesus in you might live.

I'd love to hear about what God has spoken to you and the resurrection that is taking place in your life as you've chosen to obey. While I can't answer every letter, it would be my honor to pray for you. You can reach me through my Web site contact page at www.joannaweaverbooks.com or write me at

Joanna Weaver

PO Box 607

Hamilton, MT 59840

What an amazing adventure and privilege it is to live for God. I'm so grateful we've had a chance to share this part of our lives together. My prayer for you is that God might finish the work He began in you at salvation (Philippians 1:6)—bringing you out of your tomb, unwinding your graveclothes, and transforming your life with a Lazarus awakening. Enabling you to live free and out loud for Him in such a way that the world stands up and takes notice!

I love you, dear friend. I can't wait to meet you on that day we see Jesus face to face. Until then, let's dedicate ourselves to...

Becoming His,

Joanna